LOVE,

LEADERSHIP,

& INFLUENCE

THE POWER OF TRANSFORMING RELATIONSHIPS

D1211285

Penny Tucci

FIRST EDITION

ISBN: 978-1-953576-12-5

Library of Congress Control Number: 2021918316

Published by

3741 Linden Avenue SE | Grand Rapids, MI 49548

Printed in the United States

Endorsements

I can't think of a more perfect book for Penny to write. Her loving friendship has enriched my life. Her genuine expression of the Father's love has brought breakthrough and healing in so many hearts. The influence that she carries to demonstrate true kingdom relationships is life-changing. As you read her book, get ready to let the love of Jesus overwhelm you and transform your life through your relationship with Him and those He brings into your life.

Marion Johnson,
Living Stones Church, Crown Point, Indiana

Like it or not, our lives affect others—for better or worse. Penny Tucci, who has spent a lifetime investing in others, is more than qualified to teach us how to live lives that matter. In *Love, Leadership & Influence* Penny provides clear, simple God-inspired truths that will help you build God-honoring relationships with the potential to change generations.

Get it...read it...live it!

Karen Matteo,
Member of Living Hope Church Dream Team, Latrobe, PA

The body of Christ is desperate to hear from authentic voices and genuine spiritual mothers, like Penny. The wisdom that she imparts is priceless. In this book, she shares how she navigated through personal hurt and disappointment, while continuing to trust God and love people. As you read this book you will see that her real-life examples of walking in purity towards God and people is the foundation that must be built in our hearts to lead people well. I was inspired, encouraged and challenged and know it will help you in your journey of life and leadership.

I'm honored to call her my friend.

Michelle Nuzzo,
Victory Family Church, Cranberry, PA

From the time I met Penny in my early twenties, almost four decades ago, she has been a major influence in my life—demonstrating God's love and modeling what it means to be a godly woman in leadership. I have witnessed the way she values relationships, making everyone feel like her best friend. Anyone that has been close to her has experienced the transforming power of God's grace; I am so honored to be one of them!

Get ready to be encouraged.

Natalie Paladin,
Bridge City Church, Pittsburgh, PA

I first met Penny ten years ago on a mission trip to China, and my life has never been the same. Penny models what she teaches. I have known her personally as a leader, mentor and friend. I am so grateful for the wisdom imparted in this book. I will be reading it again and again, reminding myself and encouraging others to join me as I love, lead and influence under my Father's smile.

Tabitha Bashta Phipps,
Living Stones Church, Crown Point, Indiana

Table of Contents

Foreword

(A word from the people who know Penny best)

As you read this book, it is not merely a teaching; it is an example of someone's life. Penny has chosen to spend her heart and mind in helping others—not just improving her own life, but rather focusing on the objective of improving others around her. She does not do this from a perspective of perfection in her own life; instead, her dependence is very much on her Heavenly Father.

At this writing, we have been married over 44 years, and I still stand amazed as I watch her in action—breaking barriers and jumping over walls into people's lives. When people think of the gift of hospitality, it's often in the narrow terms of serving others in their own homes. Penny's gift makes people feel at home with her wherever they are, even when they are with her in tender and fragile moments of life.

As I travel to churches to speak on a regular basis, inevitably the first question is, "Where's Penny?"—not because they want to hear her speak, although she is a great communicator; they just want to be with her. The generosity of her presence makes her in demand as a friend!

Could there be a better compliment to a person?

As you read her heart in these pages, please don't mistake these life lessons as ones that were easy for her to pursue; nor will they be for you.

That's precisely the point—you don't have to have certain gifts or have lived a life without detours and bumps to really make a difference in the lives of other people.

Penny walks you through the joy of thinking about others in the midst of her own challenges. Influencing others—strengthening them in their relationship with Jesus and with other people—is a high calling and a privilege. Penny has lived that. She is, in my opinion, the gold standard. As you read these pages, may her biography inspire you to influence others!

Keith Tucci,
Apostolic Team Leader, Network of Related Pastors
& Husband of Penny Tucci

Our mother has spent nearly 40 years raising eight children—refusing to see any of us as hopeless, despite evidence we sometimes gave to the contrary. Her influence in our lives remains a source of confidence and comfort because she has given her time to wade into the complexities of our struggles and doubts and still, her appraisal unfailingly falls on the side of hope.

Our mom is not only a beloved friend and confidant to all eight of her kids and their spouses and their kids, she's also one to all of our friends. Throughout my life, I have learned how rare it is for mothers and daughters to trust and believe in each other the way that my mom and I do. It is a treasure to have a mom like ours, and that is because she has rare gifts—ones that she has honed into teachable skills.

She has lived her life in a constant state of sacrifice—putting the interests of a husband, children, their spouses, grandchildren and countless others before her own. She's been an unwavering champion of our best interests and a relentless source of optimism for us to fall back on (a luxury we've all taken advantage of amidst the trials of life). Our mom has navigated the complex journey of being an ultimate authority to young children and morphing into our cherished friend as adults. Perhaps the most practical demonstration of her relational character is this: through hundreds of lives touched, decades of life lived, vast challenges faced and even many direct conflicts encountered…never has anyone in relationship with our mom, at any time, doubted that they were loved.

Stacie, Natalie, Benaiah, Emilie, Nathan, Annie, Jessie & Daniel (Tucci)

The Tucci Family

Introduction

Forty-four years ago, I walked down the aisle to marry a young man who I knew had a unique destiny. I didn't know exactly what that would look like or where we would end up throughout our lives. At only twenty-one years old, I was pretty clueless about life, marriage, parenthood, ministry, and most things.

After taking a three-day honeymoon at a little town close to home, we left our hometown immediately to travel to Tulsa, Oklahoma, where my new husband was to begin a year-long Bible training program. Keith knew he was called into the ministry, but other than that, our future was a blank slate.

That year in Tulsa would teach us a lot about faith and the Bible, though learning about life and people was still on the future horizon. After that year, our journey began in earnest, and over the next forty years we would pastor several churches, understanding more and more as we went. There were wonderful, heart-warming times and also incredibly painful and discouraging times. We saw the best of ministry and also some of the most challenging sides.

I still remember the many times, having felt as though we were deeply connected to a person or family, that we would see them abruptly leave, separating themselves not only from the church, but from our friendship as well. I think I never quite got used to that—always tending to open my heart wide to people, sometimes to find that they had discovered our imperfections or had taken offense at something or someone and no longer wanted to be part of our lives or our church.

I have to say though, in spite of those painful times, I am left with a sense of great appreciation and honor at having been afforded the opportunity to have a place of influence in the lives of others. Influence is a wonderful thing, if used for good. I was given the privilege of investing in and even helping to shape the lives of many precious people of all ages.

If I were to sum up my forty plus years of ministry, I would say that I deeply loved it—good and bad times notwithstanding.

Over the years, people have shared with me that they feel as though I have a gift for connecting with all types of people, for drawing them in and creating a space of community, service, and love.

My later work in the ministry has largely been about helping women understand God's heart toward them, thus being able to duplicate that in their interactions with others. I have also come alongside other pastor's wives and various women in leadership to assist in developing this atmosphere within their own churches and leadership teams.

Romans 12:9 (MSG) has been an inspirational and foundational verse that I strive to live out. It summarizes my heart-felt desire to live a life of fearless love toward God and people.

"Love from the center of who you are; don't fake it...Be good friends who love deeply."

My book contains the principles that have helped me to move in that direction, step by step, one day at a time. It wasn't easy at times. I battled a deep sense of insignificance that only the truth of God's Word was able to penetrate. An encounter with that truth changed me and taught me to live in a way I never thought I could. My hope is that you are encouraged by these words and that you feel God's smile and empowerment as you read them.

These principles or character traits open doors of influence for us in every sphere of life. They give us the ability to connect with people and build lasting and strong friendships. They help us to know God, experience His love, and readily share that love with those around us.

For those of us in ministry, they are foundational for not only being effective, but for absolutely loving what we do!

CHAPTER 1

The Power of a Pure Conscience

I'd like to open with a story that illustrates the type of struggles that seem to have had a consistent presence in my life for many years. This particular situation, and so many others with a similar underlying cause, have attempted to define me for as long as I can remember. I have so often lived with a feeling of insignificance and have responded by allowing that to determine my choices and my actions.

Many times, I felt that my life would be one void of purpose and that I would feel perpetually afraid and under the weight of unconquerable sin and shortcomings.

I chose the topic in this chapter as a starting point intentionally. I believe that, had I not discovered what it means to have a pure conscience, I would still be trapped in the painful cycle that I was prone to. I believe I am not alone in my struggle.

Although yours may be quite different in nature, we all have a propensity to wrestle with painful frailties in our lives. My hope is that you, like me, will be able to discover the joy of living every day with a pure conscience in spite of those frailties.

When I was 18 years old, I enrolled in a small Bible college about 30 minutes from my home. I had only been a Christian for a short time, but I wanted to be prepared for a future in which I could serve in the ministry. My mom's friends from church, who were not well off financially, put their funds together to pay for my first semester.

I started school with some sense of intimidation, not knowing anyone and definitely lacking in self-confidence. Throughout the first week there, I began to feel more and more insecure and afraid. During my second week, I went into the cafeteria and asked if I could sit next to another student. They abruptly told me that the seat was taken, and I awkwardly found my way to another table where I sat by myself.

That evening, I decided to quit school. I told myself I could not handle the feeling of being so isolated in the midst of a large group of people that I was supposed to be acclimating into normally; I just didn't have what it took to fit in. Somehow, I could not muster up the courage to step out of my comfort zone and make friends.

I called my mother from the pay phone in the dining area, with fear and trepidation. She was horribly disappointed and felt so bad about the investment that her friends had sacrificially made in me.

I also had to visit the dean of the school to let him know I was leaving. I was so nervous walking into his office; I hoped that he would not add to my sense of guilt. However, he was quite stern and told me that I would certainly regret my decision and that I was letting God down—not the best choice of words. By the time my mother picked me up the next day, I was both greatly relieved to be leaving and deeply disappointed in myself.

Those feelings turned to despair when I was alone at home the next day. I was reading the Bible and came across Revelation 2:4-5,

"But I have this against you, that you have left your first love. Therefore, remember from where you have fallen, and repent and do the deeds you did at first, or else I am coming to you and will remove your lampstand out of its place unless you repent."

In my unseasoned and vulnerable state, I took this to mean that, if I did not return immediately to that Bible school (and do the deeds I did at first) I would be lost in regard to my relationship with God, and my future would be hopeless.

Of course, I had taken this verse completely out of context and mentally run with it. Because of that, I was so taken over with discouragement, that I ultimately fell into a deep depression—which was something I had never experienced before. I thought my life was over if I did not go back, but I couldn't face returning to a place where I felt unwanted and rejected. So, in my mind, there was no answer or future for me.

It took me the best part of six months and counseling from wise Christian mentors to come out of my despair, and it was much longer before I understood that I had completely misinterpreted that verse and had believed a lie about my relationship with God and my future.

This story is one of many that attests to the deep sense of insignificance that plagued my young adult life and ultimately led to a chronic uncertainty about whether I was right with God or ever could be.

My approach in prayer then was a faithless greeting of, "Oh, God…" followed by sentiments of regret. I continued to read the Bible, and one day I found Acts 24:16,

"I do my best to maintain always a blameless conscience both before God and before men."

A conscience is commonly defined as a moral compass which approves or condemns a person's actions and affections—and mine seemed to condemn me no matter how hard I tried. Still, I longed to have a pure—a blameless—conscience, so this verse became a sort of plum line in my mind to aspire to. I wasn't yet certain how to attain it, but I wanted to try—to stop living under a cloud of shame and feeling as though I perpetually disappointed God. I no longer wanted to come to God with my hopeless list of sins.

So, how could someone with my issues not only achieve, but maintain a blameless conscience—someone who was still plagued by childhood frailties and fears; someone who often compared herself to others and found herself lacking; someone who believed she had little to offer any person, group, or dynamic? How could I come to believe that God was pleased with me?

It is not an easy, quick, or painless journey.

When I married Keith (several years after my Bible school debacle) he was in the process of training to be a pastor, and although I was battling my demons of insecurity, I wanted to be the kind of pastor's wife who loved people unreservedly, without intimidation. That is what I strove to be as we pastored several churches throughout our early years of marriage, with God as my ever-present teacher and needed helper.

All the while, Paul's declaration that he "did his best to maintain a blameless conscience with God and men" was still a clarion call for me, and I was still at the beginning of the journey toward my own blameless conscience.

After five years of being a pastor's wife, we had our first child, who would end up being the oldest of our eight beloved kids. As I look back now, my youngest nearly 25 years old, I realize I would never have been able to be a caring mother to my children without help and healing—I was too handicapped. But God...

As we raised our family, the undercurrent of insecurity continued to regularly knock at my door. Often, I would invite it in and let it settle into my mind, and each time I did, it would bring pain into my home—for me, for my husband, for my kids.

There were times when I would leave in the middle of a family gathering and hide in my room, feeling unpreferred and out of place, leaving my children to wrestle with their own insecurities about what they'd done to make me leave. In reality, I was deeply loved and honored by my family, but I had opened the door to that familiar feeling of insignificance, and once inside, it had clouded my perceptions, drudging up thoughts of how unimportant and unwanted I was.

It was those same thoughts that had prevailed during my short stay at Bible college, and I would respond the same way: I'd become paralyzed with fear. I'd look for a way to escape. I'd isolate myself with that feeling and let it overwhelm me.

Eventually, after being reminded how cherished I was, I would return back to the gathering and apologize to my family, realizing that I had hurt them. As much as I hated my behavior, I was prone to repeat it each time I felt undesirable. Thus, another discouraged beseeching of God: "Oh God, I've done it again..." My conscience remained impure, burdened.

Often, I felt I would never get over my weaknesses or stop my immature behaviors. I wondered if I'd ever feel at peace or secure. My cry was Jeremiah 15:18,

> "Why is my pain unending and my wound incurable, refusing
> to be healed?"

Eventually, I would discover that the answer is given in the very next verse, which has now become a life verse for me:

> "Therefore, thus says the Lord, If you return to Me (and give

up this mistaken tone of distrust, despair and self-pity), then I will give you again a settled place of quiet and safety, and you will be My minister; and if you separate the precious from the vile (cleansing your own heart from unworthy and unwarranted suspicions concerning God's faithfulness) you shall be my mouthpiece." (Jeremiah 15:19, AMP)

Ultimately, this is where I would find my settled place of quiet from all the tormenting, distorting thoughts. This is where I would find safety. This is where my incurable wound would become healed. How? By learning to lean on the loving arm of my Heavenly Father and letting His view of me influence my own—by returning again and again to His tender heart toward me and His ability to give me courage.

In the Bible's original language, the word conscience means "to see together with" or "a joint-knowing." In other words, the conscience is derived from our ability to see properly together with God. I had been used to just seeing my weakness, my sin, my fear from a misguided perspective that gave God no opportunity to weigh in. But, when we allow Him and His Word to enlighten our thinking, we see things differently. We see things clearly. We see things with hope.

Without God, we wouldn't have a conscience. He defines what is good and right, and what isn't. Thankfully, He is always willing to look at things with us and then help us work through any problem, sin, or situation.

The more I invite Him into my thought processes and mullings, the more I have clarity and wisdom to do things in a redemptive way. Instead of being drawn into a vortex of doubt and self-rejection, I am encouraged to see myself through His eyes. I have learned a great deal about what the Bible says about God's viewpoints, perspectives, and perceptions of me and of others. That has enabled me to reject the subjective thoughts that would seek to keep me beat down and disabled.

I've come to realize on a personal level that, while God doesn't give us a pass for our sin and failures, He gives us a hand up in overcoming them.

I have gradually learned to see God in a very different light than I did when I would approach Him as a disapproving, disappointed master. I have accepted His invitation to be his beloved child. In Romans 8:15 we find that *"We have received the Spirit of adoption, whereby we cry out, 'Abba Father.'"* The name Abba is a tender and intimate word—it actually is the word for daddy.

Having grown up with a father who left our family when I was 13 and who was not involved in my life after that, I had to go beyond my natural inclinations in order to see God as a legitimate father. I couldn't even relate to a father much at all, let alone think that God could be a cherishing, nurturing one. I had to study to find God's character and nature as it truly is, thus rejecting my false ideas.

I began to look up Bible verses that spoke of God's fatherhood. I purchased inspirational books about God's heart as a father. I pursued God in a relentless way, asking Him to show me in His Word and in my heart what it means to have a real dad.

Throughout the last many years, God has become my Abba—my dad—my true father. I am no longer an orphan, but rather a cherished daughter, able to ask my Father anything without scorn or negative scrutiny.

One unique and surprising story happened over twenty years ago when my youngest son was two years old. Our home at the time was in a beautiful community on thirty acres and situated at the bottom of a steep driveway. One day I had walked up to the top of that scenic driveway, as was often my custom, to pray.

While talking to God about my struggle to believe I was valuable, I sensed that He was asking me to consider myself as His beloved princess—the daughter of a King. I told him out loud that I found that description to be very unnatural to me. I felt a persistent voice in my spirit urging me to think in a new way and take that encouragement to heart. I told God I would try.

After an hour or so talking and reasoning with the Lord, I began to walk down to my house. When I was about fifty feet away, my adorable two-year old son came running out the door. We always were close, and to have him run and jump into my arms was nothing out of the ordinary. What he said when I reached and picked him up was another story: as I was lifting him up, he looked me right in the eye and said, "My princess." Utterly shocked, I said, "What did you say?" He repeated it again, "My princess." I was stunned; he had never used that terminology before or called me anything but mommy.

The Lord has a way of getting His message across and showing us in the most tender and profound ways that we are His, and we are cherished, and that we actually can and do hear His voice.

Although I was given a unique opportunity to embrace God's reminder that I am His princess, He is looking to communicate that message to you as well. Are you willing to consider that He, being the King of the Universe, has called you to be his beloved daughter—His princess?

He is always inviting us to come close to Him—to have our conscience made pure—and creating an avenue for us to see Him as our unchanging Father, who calls us His very own beloved children. Hebrews 10:22 tells us that we can,

> "...draw near with a true heart in full assurance of faith, and
> have our hearts sprinkled clean from an evil conscience."

My heart stays near to Him because I do not improperly fear Him. I love Him and know Him and trust Him.

I no longer have to limp by with a crippled or hardened conscience, thinking there is no real way to please Him. I have come to understand that as long as I *"believe that He is and that He is a rewarder of those who diligently seek Him"* (Hebrews 11:6), I can simply come to Him with every need, weakness, and sin. He affirms me, while showing me how to overcome sin and to face life with hope.

Now, I don't start my prayer with a downcast, "Oh, God…." Instead, I look up into His eyes with confidence and security—not doubting His feelings and intentions toward me, no longer afraid that I need to be perfect in order to be close to Him.

God desires to have a warm and genuine relationship with His children.

Have you ever taken the time to consider what qualities make the best earthly father? Having not experienced that as a child, I have had to observe others in order to understand what it looks like.

I've watched my husband sacrifice for, serve, and undyingly love our children while remaining faithful to them, whether or not they follow his mandates and hopes for their lives. No matter their shortcomings or even opposing choices, his love or willingness to give his all for them does not change.

I have observed fathers who demonstrate many different traits that would be considered those of a great father. If you take them all and put them together in one person, that would not even come close to the type of father our heavenly father is.

He invented fatherhood—and motherhood—and embodies all the qualities of both. The strength and vigilance of a father, the nurturing and tenderness of a mother: that can all be found in His character and personality.

A. W. Tozer, a theologian from the mid 1900s, said, "What comes into our minds when we think about God is the most important thing about us." I completely agree. It will define us and color all of our decisions. It will give us courage and empower us or it will discourage and defeat us.

Could it be that you, like I had done, have misjudged God's character or his overall mindset toward you? Do you feel encouraged, strengthened and empowered when you think of God and His demeanor toward you? Or do you feel discouraged, guilty and defeated when pondering God's thoughts toward you?

2 Peter 1:2 tells us that,

"Grace and peace will be multiplied to us through the true, accurate and intimate knowledge of God and of Jesus our Lord."

This verse is specifically communicating that we can have God's grace—which is His ability—and His peace. However, that only comes through a knowledge of Him that is accurate, personal and intimate— not speculative, ill-informed head knowledge.

Is your knowledge of God one that is personal, intimate, and based on truth—having been acquired through a thorough and consistent study of the Bible and time alone with Him? Or, rather, has your knowledge of God been even partially acquired through rumor, speculation, and second-hand information? Many people are unable to trust God because they have heard about Him from someone who misrepresented Him or because of tragedies they've witnessed and assumed that He was responsible for.

Again, if we were referring to our earthly father, we would be hard pressed to find security in him if we were distant from him and misinformed. If asked to throw ourselves at his mercy and trust that he'd care for us, we would be unwilling without the assurance a close and proven relationship would provide. At best, we'd be apprehensive to depend on him; but imagine if we'd heard rumors that he was a harsh, judgmental, cold and calculated man who punishes everyone who steps out of line.

However, if we knew his consistent, faithful, forgiving, dependable, and kind character toward those that call Him Father, we could easily have confidence in Him and be at peace about how He would handle things that concern us.

We have to get this right—it will chart our course and determine our destiny. When you come to understand God's character and His heart toward you in a way that no one can ever steal from you, then you are on your way to living with a blameless conscience.

It's important to remember that having a blameless conscience and being sinless are not the same. One is about having our hearts sprinkled clean consistently and living under the gratifying place of peace which results from that. The other is an impossible objective that no mere mortal has yet attained.

During my journey to better know Him as my true Father, God has spoken to my heart that, as His daughter, I live under His perpetual smile. Again, this doesn't mean I have arrived as a perfect person who doesn't need to be adjusted, corrected, challenged. It means He is the ultimate Father, smiling on me even when He is correcting me.

Think of the demeanor of a patient, doting parent whose child has just stolen several cookies from a forbidden jar: does that parent suddenly become irate and disapproving, unable to cherish and adore that child because she has disobeyed? Rather, He comes to the child and brings loving correction, with a smile in his heart toward her.

Many of us need to rethink our perception of God, even if we can confidently say that we know God loves us. What does that mean? Where are the limits to that love? How is that love demonstrated? Must it be earned by behavior that is acceptable?

Those are questions that we all need to consider. I would encourage you to take some time and ask yourself what you believe about God's attitude and demeanor toward you.

I do not mean to say that God cares not about our sin or our choices. He most certainly does. But His disposition does not change with our behaviors. His love is enduring and strong—bringing about the changes that we thought we were incapable of making. Romans 2:4 makes it clear that it is *"His kindness that leads us to repentance,"* not His judgment, His disapproval, or His punishing distance from us.

A quote from a favorite book of mine, *Abba's Child*, says,

> Define yourself radically as one beloved by God. This is the
> true self. Every other identity is an illusion.

This has become the place where I live. This is my foundation. This is my abode. Even in the most unsettling of moments, when I am struggling with insecurity or any number of weaknesses I possess, I have chosen to return again and again to this place of safety and refuge, which is what Jeremiah 15:19 so clearly encourages us to do. This is where I am heard, forgiven and empowered to become like Jesus. This understanding is my impetus for living and loving.

About fifteen years ago, I was at a retreat spending time reading the Bible and listening for God's voice. As I was reading Isaiah chapter 62, verse 3 seemed to stand out very strongly to me. It reads, *"You shall be a crown of beauty in the hand of the Lord..."* I wrote it in my journal, sensing that the Lord was trying to convey His perception of me.

Strongly encouraged by that, I thought about it often over the next several weeks. Months later, I was attending a church service and went forward to ask for prayer for a specific need. While praying for me, the pastor's wife spoke to me saying, "God says you are a crown of beauty in the hand of the Lord."

That became a defining moment, again confirming my Heavenly Father's estimation of how He sees me. I held fast to that and have continued to inquire about how that truth affects my decisions, my attitudes, my relationships, and my personality. So many facets continue to be opened up to me as I rest in His overarching pronouncement and vision for me. I have a deep sense of what that verse means and how it guides my life.

Rather than assume God's judgment, anger, or disfavor, I continually see myself as *His Crown of Beauty* who lives under His smile and favor. All of my failures and sin will be eradicated through that lens and with that as my springboard, as I fearlessly allow Him to instruct and change me.

I no longer go around with a sullied conscience. Instead, I can hold my head high and face any struggle or even personal character weakness from a place of favor and ability.

My faith is rooted deeply in His great love and care for me. I have the courage to face any person, any opportunity, any dilemma under that smile. It is the banner over my life. I look up regularly to see the face of my true Father, my dad, my refuge, my redeemer, my hope—and He is always smiling.

Do you want to live under the perpetual smile of God? You can! Will you be sinless or perfect? No. But you will be His beloved child, drawing near to Him with a true heart in full assurance of faith, consistently having your heart "sprinkled clean from an evil conscience."

In chapter two, we will talk about the most basic and critical principle of connecting with God.

CHAPTER 2

The Power of Faith

Without faith in our lives, we are hard pressed to live a life that is meaningful and fruitful. The Bible clearly teaches us, over and over again, that we cannot please God without faith. We cannot even come to a place of surrender to Him—salvation—without faith. Ephesians 2:8 bears this out.

> "For by grace you have been saved through faith, and that not
> of yourselves; it is the gift of God."

I have been learning what it looks like to live by faith in God from the time I first surrendered my life to Him, at the age of 17. Even at my young age, I had already clearly seen that I could not live a life that was purposeful or enjoyable. Instead, I was hitting one wall after another, struggling to make sense of what my life was meant for.

As I began to live with a radically changed perspective, I sought to know what this God—this savior—who I had embraced was like. I would spend a great deal of time studying the Bible and praying alone in my bedroom. I was always one who loved alone time, and now that time became very intentional and enjoyable.

I truly felt the friendship that Jesus spoke of from that first day as a believer. I would talk to God very openly and wait to hear His response, which would resonate in my heart. I journaled, memorized verses, and asked for help with everything in my life. I was soon to find out that God was able to help and to instruct me.

It's interesting how we, as new Christians, seem to have an innate confidence in God—we've not yet talked ourselves out of the pure and innocent trust in God's ability to do whatever we need whenever we ask.

Hebrews 11 is an overview of what faith looks like and how it operates. It begins by letting us know that *"faith is the certainty of things hoped for, a proof of things not seen."* In other words, we begin by hoping and, when we apply faith in God's ability to make our hope a reality, we can see the outcome or proof of that thing come to pass.

It goes on to describe how God made the world by speaking it into being with faith-filled words, knowing that what He was speaking would surely happen. From there, many examples are given of people responding to an invisible God with faith-filled obedience.

In verse 6, there is a very telling and clear-cut statement.

"Without faith it is impossible to please Him, for the one who comes to God must believe that He exists, and that He proves to be the One who rewards those who seek Him."

That is an unavoidable, foundational, doctrinal standard that lays out a principle that is meant to guide all of our actions. As His child, I desire to please Him. It is apparent from this verse that the only real way to do that is for me to have and apply faith.

I'd like to give some clarity to my understanding of how this works in my life. I have found that the greatest thing I do to please and connect with God is to take Him at His word. If the Bible promises something, when I embrace that promise as being absolute, honorable, and utterly true, I make God happy.

He deeply values our willingness to understand that His integrity is rock solid and that He has declared,

"For I know the plans that I have for you, declares the Lord, plans for prosperity and not for disaster, to give you a future and a hope." (Jeremiah 29:11)

I don't always know how this is going to play out, and the realization of something I am hoping for is often not immediate.

But, in returning again and again to the belief that He is everything His Word says and that He does everything He promises, I align myself with God's greatest desire—people who trust Him with all of our hearts.

"Trust in the Lord with all your heart and do not lean on your own understanding. In all your ways acknowledge Him and He will direct your path." (Proverbs 3:5-6)

I have not seen all of my prayers answered. There are things that I do not understand and may never understand on this earth. I know that I see things from a limited perspective, so I am not looking to condemn people or myself for not having "enough faith." I have certainly not received many things that are very important to me and am still processing what the next step is in those areas.

Perhaps you have seen some or even many of your prayers go unanswered. Perhaps you have become discouraged, thinking God is not interested in you or your needs. I know the temptation to misunderstand or even misjudge God based on the circumstances around us.

These are the times when we need to look deeper into God's Word and His promises for us. Although it may seem unclear at the moment, perseverance is so important and will ultimately lead to greater clarity and to hope.

Romans 5 talks about trials and difficulties. In verse 4 we see that those trials produce perseverance and proven character in us and ultimately, bring hope when we persevere. Then in verse 5, we find that *"hope does not disappoint us, because the love of God has been poured out in our hearts."*

There are some things that are clear and that resonate with me. One of those things is that I will continue to persevere in my ability to trust Him and His good plan and good intention for me. I will attempt to allow His promises to be my pathway for having my needs met.

2 Peter 1:4 gives us a clear-cut and inspiring plan for receiving from God. It says,

"He has granted to us His precious and magnificent promises. So that by them you may become partakers of the divine nature, having escaped the corruption that is in the world by lust."

That tells me that there is a way to be more like Him—to be *"partakers of the divine nature."*

What is that way? To receive and hold onto His promises for all types of things in my life—for my day-to-day needs, for relational and emotional struggles, for health issues, for financial needs, and for so much more. So, not only does He promise to take care of me and the things that I need, He says He will make me more like Him as I learn to believe those promises are true and available for me—that's a pretty great trade off! He says, rather than lusting for the things that I need, I can learn to pray for them and believe He will respond to me in the midst of that belief.

I understand that these principles are learned throughout a lifetime and not just automatically imparted. But, I also want to continue to learn… to be a person who knows God is for me and working on my behalf and that I can trust Him for everything I am in need of.

In line with that, I will not falsely charge Him when things go awry and blame Him for things He is not responsible for. Often, people shun God and refuse to come near Him because they hold Him responsible for great loss or dysfunction in their lives or in the lives of others.

They perhaps have yet to experience or recognize the depth of the unending, tender lovingkindness that He longs to demonstrate—even when we struggle to see it or to believe that it is real. I have had times where that realization was hard to grasp—when I wasn't sure if I would survive the trial I was facing.

When I eventually looked up to see His smile and His hand reaching out to help me, I found the courage to face whatever the hardship was at that time. Around the next bend was often a great breakthrough or even a miraculous answer to prayer.

David knew the amazing ability of God to bring breakthrough. After a perilous battle, he said,

"The Lord has broken through my enemies before me, like a breakthrough of water. So he named that place Baal-perazim" (Master of the breakthrough). (2 Samuel 5:20)

God is the master of our breakthrough!

There will always be things that are unexplainable to us—that seem so unfair and cruel. It is obvious to me that we live in a world that has fallen and is not the original perfect garden that was planned for us. In this fallen world, things go horribly wrong and many times fall apart. We battle enemies that we cannot see and whose determination and objectives we underestimate.

1 Peter 5:8 warns us,

"Be of sober spirit, be on the alert. Your adversary, the devil, prowls around like a roaring lion, seeking someone to devour."

In John 10:10, God attempts to both alert us of Satan's intention and to clarify His own:

"The thief comes only to steal, kill and destroy. I came that they might have life and might have it abundantly."

Faith is an unfolding gift that spreads itself underneath us and lifts us up to be able to not only face an obstacle or tragedy, but to see an answer, a solution—a breakthrough. Faith, held onto, can turn things around and bring a miracle our way. Faith is vital to all that we do and everything we hope for.

I'm still learning. I'm still attempting to apply the truth of God's promises to my daily life. As I do, I can, without a doubt, tell you that I have seen more answers to prayer than I can tell of. Often, I feel unsteady and afraid. In those moments, I try to remember that God has a promise with my name on it. I look up and speak that promise over my life and my future. I see the breakthrough time and time again.

I'd like to close this chapter by including Psalm 91, a familiar chapter to many. Faith is based on something that is clearly promised; it does not occur in a vacuum. God's promises contained in His Word are the foundation for our faith. They become the basis for our hope. I've written it in the first person, because I take it very personally, as if it is written very much with me in mind. As you read it, I hope you see it personally as well and realize afresh how tenderly and consistently He looks out for us—protecting us and fulfilling our lives.

"I dwell in the shelter of the Most High and I abide in the shadow of the Almighty. I will say to the Lord, 'You are my refuge and my fortress, my God, in whom I trust.' For it is You who delivers me from the snare of the trapper and from the deadly pestilence. You will cover me with your pinions and under Your wings I will seek refuge.

Your faithfulness is a shield and a defensive wall. I will not be afraid of the terror by night or of the arrow that flies by day, of the pestilence (defined: pandemic) that stalks in darkness, or of the destruction that lays waste at noon. A thousand may fall at my side and ten thousand at my right hand, but it shall not approach me.

I will only look on with my eyes and see the recompense of the wicked. For I have made the Lord, my refuge, even the Most High, my dwelling place. No evil will befall me, nor will any plague come near my tent. For He will give His angels charge concerning me to guard me in all my ways. They will bear me up in their hands, so that I will not strike my foot against a stone. I will tread upon the lion and cobra, the young lion and serpent I will trample down.

Because You have loved me, therefore You will deliver me; You will set me securely on high, because you have known my name. I will call upon You and You will answer me. You will be with me in trouble. You will rescue me and honor me. With a long life You will satisfy me and let me see Your salvation." (Psalm 91)

God wants you to put all of your hope and confidence in Him—in His care for you and in His promises to you. If you learn to do that, your life will be both purposeful and fulfilling. I find Him to be completely trustworthy, willing to reward my faith in Him at every turn. There is no other way to please Him—faith in His unchanging character is the way!

In chapter 3, I talk about an impossible situation in my life, which became a miracle as I mixed faith with forgiveness.

The Power of Forgiveness

Much has been written about the topic of forgiveness. Life affords us so many opportunities to forgive. Of course, we have the choice to refuse to forgive, holding onto the offense and hurt instead, which inevitably leads to bitterness.

I have a little test I give myself to help determine whether I may have any unforgiveness toward an individual. If any of the following symptoms are present, there's a very good chance I am harboring unforgiveness: avoidance, disdain, being cynical and critical toward them, feeling irritated or annoyed by hearing their voice. This is a practical and simple check-up we can give ourselves.

Do any of these symptoms seem familiar? Do you have one or maybe more persons in your life that you tend to avoid? Perhaps there is someone in your family or even your spouse. Maybe you have become accustomed to these feelings and reactions. This may be a good time to reexamine your relationships and allow God's influence to change the way you see some of them.

These types of feelings may seem very justified in our thinking, and at face value, they may well be. Psalm 32 has been a reminder to me of what happens in my own life and soul when I allow things, like unforgiveness, to go unchecked.

"How blessed is he whose transgression is forgiven, whose sin is covered...When I kept quiet about my sin, my body wasted away, through my groaning all day long, for day and night Your hand was heavy upon me. My vitality drained away as with the fever heat of summer.

Then, I acknowledged my sin to You and my sin I did not hide; I said, 'I will confess my transgressions to the Lord; and You forgave the guilt of my sin...You surrounded me with songs of deliverance...He who trusts in the Lord, lovingkindness shall surround him."

When I am avoiding someone, or viewing them with disdain, I feel heavy in a part of my heart. I have an unsettledness that tells me that something is amiss and that I need to look deeper at what it may be. When I am holding onto unforgiveness, even subconsciously, I lose part of my joy.

When my conscience is unhindered, I often go around singing and talking to God out loud, without hindrance. But, when something is off, there is no longer a song in my heart...rather, I feel flat and somewhat discouraged. This is like an engine light that comes on in a car when it needs maintenance and attention—my conscience is reminding me that I need to pay attention to an area that I may be avoiding.

There is a joke that I like to tell that illustrates this. My kids always tease me about my humor (or lack thereof), but I would not want to prevent you from partaking in what I consider a great joke:

There was a woman who had a pet bird that she dearly loved. It became so ill that it fell on its side and was no longer moving. She was hoping that the bird would somehow come around, so she took it to the veterinarian. He examined the bird and gently told the woman that the bird had died.

She just refused to believe it. She asked for a second opinion. The vet offered to bring his pet cat into the exam room and have it look the bird over. The woman agreed, and the cat sniffed the bird thoroughly. Looking up, it let out a plaintive "meooooow", indicating that it concurred with the vet—the bird was indeed dead.

The owner of the bird was still unconvinced, so the vet offered one more option to confirm the diagnosis. He told her that he could bring in his pet Labrador Retriever who was familiar with birds—living and dead. The woman welcomed that final opportunity in hopes that the Lab would disagree with the vet and his cat. The Labrador gently sniffed the bird, only to offer a sad, whiny growl, indicating a unanimous decision: the bird was gone.

After finally coming to terms with the loss, she asked the veterinarian for her bill. He handed her an invoice for $1,000.00. She looked shocked and exclaimed, "How could your bill be this high just to examine my little bird!"

He explained, "Oh, well my bill was $100.00; the remainder was for the cat scan and the lab report!"

I actually enjoy this joke a great deal—even if my family is not amused by it. You see, the ability to talk to my Father freely and sing as I go about my day as opposed to feeling distant and disconnected is like a cat scan and a lab report for my heart—indicating life or death— reminding me that I need to take inventory of what is at play.

We can bury hurt and unforgiveness in such a way that we are blind to the fact that it exists in our hearts.

I have come to realize, on a personal level, that bitterness can be veiled by callousness and indifference. It doesn't have to be demonstrated by blatant, angry displays or be observable to others at all.

A friend of mine who was in her early twenties at the time, relayed a story about herself to me. She told me about a method whereby she would choose who she would and would not allow access into her life. She said that she had compiled a mental inventory of those who had let her down, insulted her, embarrassed her, hurt her, or crossed her in any manner. On this secret inventory, as people would offend her in various ways, she would take note and put a mental check mark by their name.

At the time that she shared this story with me, she had eliminated all but two people within her sphere of relationship—having decided that none of the others were worthy of her trust. It's notable that none of those that she had mentally excommunicated from her good graces was aware of it. She had continued to demonstrate an outward appearance of good manners and even good humor toward them, often even complimenting them and laughing with them. It was an internal decision and an internal disconnect. The outward behavior was merely a front, in order to make sure no one saw her actual feelings.

She was a person with a great deal of secret internal indifference toward people around her, but in truth, she had bitterness and unforgiveness toward them.

So, unforgiveness can be disguised in different forms, but no matter what form it takes, it leaves an effect on both the person who possesses it and the person to whom it is directed. The greater effect is often upon the one who has allowed it to take up residence in their heart, although we can be completely unaware of how we are being affected.

One such situation involved my relationship with my father. He was never very involved in my life. He spent a good bit of time at work, and when he was available, he was taken up with his own personal hobbies and interests. Having come from a home where his own father had been unfaithful in both of his marriages, my dad followed suit and had a propensity toward falling for women other than my mother. One such woman came on the scene when I was thirteen years old.

I had just started high school and was experiencing a great many changes in my life. Friendships at that age can be difficult to navigate and there was some painful drama with my friend group. Needless to say, life was not falling into place for me at the tender age of thirteen.

One afternoon, as I walked into the house after school, I found my mother weeping. I rarely saw her this upset, so I knew something devastating had happened. When I asked, she explained through her sobs that my father had left us all to live with a neighbor of ours, whom he had only recently met. Her husband had been killed in a trucking accident just weeks before this time; my mom had actually been at her home when she received the news of his death.

A short while later, in an effort to help and encourage her, my mother invited her to a small party for a few friends at our home. She struck up a conversation with my dad that evening and asked him to drive her home. Throughout the next month, they became romantically involved and very quickly thereafter, he announced to my mom that he was leaving her for this woman.

Listening to my mom's broken-hearted words that afternoon, I struggled to believe it could be true. I was only 13 and had no idea that this had been going on. I knew my parents didn't always get along, but I was completely unaware of my dad's propensity and his involvement with this woman. Although he had been largely absent in the role of a father, I still felt the betrayal very deeply, both for my mom and for myself.

My dad had traded his entire family in for an attractive neighbor—a friend of my mother—who he had just recently met! He no longer cared about being my dad or being a part of my life.

Throughout the weeks to come, my initial shock turned to rage. The more I saw my mom's pain, the angrier I got. I was deeply impacted and hurt, even though I would not readily admit it. Instead, I responded with anger. I was infuriated with both my father and the woman. I found very clear ways to demonstrate my immense anger.

I walked past her home frequently, making sure that I loudly spouted off hateful sentiments, in hopes that she would hear them. When I had the chance occasion to see my father, I made sure I told him what a horrible person his newfound love interest was. I was seething with intense hatred and took joy in making it known to him. My attitude toward him for the next several years remained one of obvious hateful disdain and utter rejection of any type of relationship with him.

When I turned seventeen, I had the life-changing experience of receiving Jesus Christ as my personal lord, savior, and friend. I began to quickly change as a person, and part of that change was trading in my deep anger toward my father for a type of resignation and the beginnings of forgiveness.

I became much more tender-hearted toward my mother and others in my life, whom I had formerly been indifferent or even unkind to. I began to see behaviors that had seemed acceptable in the past through a new lens and realized that I had actually been rude and hurtful, and much of the time, I had lacked any genuine concern for others.

I became a different person on that spring day in 1975. It was undeniable—everyone saw the complete and utter change in me. God had done what He promised in 2 Corinthians 5:17,

"If anyone is in Christ, he is a new creature; Old things are passed away and all things are made new."

Although my overall disposition toward my dad did change in a very real way, there was still an awkward distance between us. I had reacted to his abandonment much more strongly than my brother and sisters. They were able to maintain a relationship with him to some degree; I had refused to. But I wanted to reopen my heart to him, despite the nagging feeling that I was and always had been less loved by him than my three siblings were.

At one point while he was living several states away, I attempted to meet him a few hours from his new home, but he declined my invitation and remained largely uninterested in relating to me. When he occasionally made trips to visit our home state of Pennsylvania, he never made it a priority to see me, even as he met with my siblings. These and other things further convinced me that I was unimportant to him.

I tried to chalk it up to fallout from my former displays of rage toward him. I tried to ignore it, move on, and just live my life without his involvement; however, it would become apparent, even in my dreams, that it was still haunting my mind. I would dream that I was sitting beside him at a social event and he would turn away from me while I was speaking to him and completely ignore me.

Another recurring dream would find me knocking at his door in an attempt to visit him. He reluctantly allowed me into his home but made a point of showing me his family photo wall, with many photos of my siblings and none of me. I had other dreams as well, and the idea that I was his least favorite never left the back of my mind.

Throughout the next twenty-five years, I could count on one hand the times that I saw and interacted with my dad. After my initial attempts to see him, I had determined that I would no longer be the pursuer, but that, if he was interested in being a part of my life, he would have to make it clear. That was not to be the case.

I had convinced myself that, because I didn't sit around and consciously dwell on my feelings toward him, I had forgiven him and it needed to go no further. I had survived thus far without his involvement in my life—why feel the need for that to change?

To illustrate the level of contact I had with my father, he stopped to visit twice that I recall throughout the entire time we were raising our eight children. As a matter of fact, one of those two times, he actually stopped by my home, and my kids came running in to tell me that there was an older man in our driveway. They had no idea who he was; they did not know him at all. This whole dynamic disturbed me greatly, as I had always wanted them to have a doting grandfather; Keith's father was also uninvolved. But, suffice it to say, we were anything but close. We were estranged.

At one point, when life was full of responsibility and activity, Keith and I decided to go away to a Christian retreat center. We wanted to spend time together, to get a break and also to try to get a greater understanding of some stumbling blocks we were experiencing in our marriage.

While we were there, the director of the retreat center had asked to speak to me. She shared that she felt I was holding onto some issues regarding my father and it was affecting me in more ways than I understood. I decided to spend some time talking to God about it, so I found a quiet place to be alone and began to think about what she had told me.

I made a decision to revisit my feelings about my dad. What did I really think about him, especially in relation to me? I opened the door to see that I had been hurt way more deeply than I had been willing to admit—the level of my anger coincided with the level of my hurt.

When there was no opportunity to alleviate any of this pain, despite several attempts to try to work things out with my dad later on, I had chosen the refuge of apathy and indifference.

I began to consider that perhaps I had not fully forgiven my dad but had instead put a giant *"you are superfluous to my life"* mental checkmark beside his name, not even realizing that it was secretly affecting my marriage and many other things.

I decided to try to be fully honest and express anything that was hiding in the recesses of my heart to God.

I started off by considering and voicing the sense of rejection and abandonment I felt about my father leaving—him showing no regard for myself or my family, making it completely about himself. Once I opened up that door, I spared no detail. I felt like David in the Psalms—laying out the truth to God about the things my dad had done to my family and, more particularly, to me personally.

After sharing all of my hurt with God, it was important for me to make a vocal proclamation of my forgiveness—that is, to say out loud "I forgive my dad for leaving our family, for not loving me, for not favoring me, for rejecting me, and for showing no interest in my children the same way he'd shown no interest in me." I released him from the place of distance and judgment I had kept him in with my unforgiveness, and I prayed that God would bless him with favor and a loving heart. I also asked that He would make my heart tender toward my dad and help to restore our relationship.

Then I asked Him for one more thing—I asked God to give me, specifically, favor with my dad—something I'd never felt I had.

I did not feel an immediate change of heart or sense of relief, but I knew that I had been obedient to God. Three days later, we were back at home when I picked up the ringing phone to hear my father's voice. He said he wanted to come and visit for the holidays and that he had a gift for my children—the first gift he had ever given them. He was warm and engaging and actually seemed excited about coming to see us. I told him that I'd be very happy to have him visit.

Upon hanging up, I stood rather dumbfounded at what seemed to be an obvious outcome to my prayers. "Wow, God," I thought, "That was pretty amazing!"

My father did indeed come to visit, bringing $100.00 as a Christmas gift for our children and showing his first real interest in getting to know them during his five-hour visit. He asked them about themselves and their hobbies. He showed them affection and treated me as though he truly cared for me, even calling me by a childhood nickname that he had for me. I was taken aback by what was undeniably a very clear response on God's part to my prayer.

Throughout the next several months, my father began to write letters to my children, telling them how much he missed and loved them. They were sweet and tender—a part of my dad I had not previously seen. He would draw little paw prints to say hello to them from his dog.

This went on consistently over the next months, while he also began to call me to chat on a regular basis—again, a totally new thing! He even mentioned that he had considered moving back to Pennsylvania from North Carolina to be close to me and my family. What a change!

Close to a year after his initial visit, he called, asking if he could come and stay for several days. He told me that he had a special gift that he wanted to give my children and that he wanted to spend time with us. He was in his eighties and in poor health, having had several triple heart bypass surgeries and other health concerns throughout his life. He struggled with driving that far, but said he really wanted to do it anyway.

I told him we would be very happy to have him come, so within a few weeks, he arrived, suitcase in hand and wanting only to spend time with me and my family. Instead of visiting anyone else while in town, he was content to sit with me and my kids, just talking and relaxing. He had purchased a nice, portable piano keyboard as a gift for our children and brought it with him. He was so happy to be able to give them something that would remind them of him.

One day, while we were sitting outside, he told me that he was very sorry for what he had done to hurt us all—my mom included. He said he realized he had brought so much pain into our lives and had been thinking a lot about it lately.

The day before he left, I had the opportunity to affirm that he was right in his heart with God and ready for Heaven. I also asked him to speak a blessing of a father over me—having read about it in the Bible and witnessed other people receiving such a prayer. He, although a bit unsure, agreed, and I showed him what I meant. He did it sweetly and tenderly; it was short but precious.

When he finished, I asked if I could pray for him. He said, "yes," so I gently put my hand on his shoulder and prayed a short prayer of release and blessing over him (a shortened and inoffensive version of the type I had prayed on our retreat). I spoke total forgiveness over his life and release from any guilt or shame he had been carrying. At the end of the prayer, he laid his head on the table and quietly wept.

I pondered that visit over and over, realizing that I had just witnessed one of the most specific and miraculous answers to prayer that I had ever seen personally. God had taken my sincere, not overly passionate prayer and turned it into a life-changing event, which from that day forward colored my relationship with my father in a totally different light.

What had been rejection and insignificance in my father's eyes now had become favor and love. What had been sour and bitter became sweet and joyful. What was hard-hearted and dark inside the very inner part of my spirit became tender and full of light.

My forever perspective in regard to my father was changed, never to be revisited by the brokenness that once was. I was now a beloved daughter—free from any and all bitterness and unforgiveness in relation to my father. What a gift! Who could have known that a simple prayer would lead to a tremendous change in my life!

In an unexpected and very sad turn of events, my father passed away a short month after his visit, due to health conditions that I mentioned previously. He was quite ill, even during his visit with us, but God, in His love and mercy for us both, orchestrated a restoration that has deeply touched my life.

After my father died, I was able to feel deep sorrow, having just recently gained the precious emergence of an actual father/daughter relationship. I now had genuinely lost something dear to my heart, which I had not previously been an obvious recipient of—the love and favor of my earthly father.

I was asked to speak at his funeral. I shared our story and how God had brought about such a wonderful healing. I spoke of how *"He will return the hearts of the fathers back to the children and the hearts of the children to their fathers…"* (Malachi 4:6).

I also realized that, although I thought I'd had no bitterness toward my father before that day at the retreat center, it had been there all along, hidden behind coldness and indifference.

Bitterness doesn't have to be full of passion and outbursts of anger; it can be a suppressed and quiet "writing off" of an individual in order to avoid further pain or rejection. Although the motive may seem innocuous and even necessary, bitterness will still create a prison and self-perpetuating protection for ourselves that doesn't allow for vulnerability.

I learned that bitterness and unforgiveness need to be confronted in a way that is proactive and definitive. They need to be acknowledged and brought into the light of what they really are. They need to be brought into the life-altering place of faith, where God can do something beyond our imagination with our willingness to relinquish them in a clear and unmistakable way—trading them in for release and blessing instead.

This experience also set the stage for my ability to adopt the understanding of being a beloved daughter to my Heavenly Father—another life-changing realization that has completely transformed me.

So many people have painful, disconnected relationships with their fathers, for any number of reasons. Perhaps you can relate in many ways to my story. Have you been hurt or rejected by your father or perhaps your mother? Maybe you have responded to the loss in a similar manner as I did? Have you closed off your heart and written them off, thinking it's better to just ignore the hurt associated with your relationship with them?

My hope is to inspire you to rethink how you have responded to painful relationships. My experience has changed my personal life and has given me a great catalyst for hope and peace.

Unforgiveness—even when it is buried beneath apathy—affects us.

When we acknowledge it and choose active, purposeful forgiveness, there is a genuine change. While I cannot guarantee the same miraculous outcome that I had in regard to my own father, the Bible calls us to forgive from our hearts.

I have had the privilege of helping many people walk through a process of forgiveness toward people in their lives. I have shown them how to openly talk to God about their situation — acknowledging and describing the reason and level of hurt and offense they have felt. They faced their pain and then made a clear and willful choice to forgive, release and bless those same individuals. The freedom in their own hearts from doing so has been immediate and very real. The outcome in relationships has also been impactful.

The story of the change in my relationship with my earthly father is one of many times that I have chosen forgiveness—sometimes not without first suffering the repercussions of a hard heart and having no other alternative than to finally give in and forgive. Upon doing so, I have seen an outcome that is reflective of the verse in Jeremiah 15:19 that tells us to return to God and trade our ill-directed suspicions about His faithfulness, in for trust and wholeness instead, thus finding ourselves in a settled, quiet and fruitful place.

An area that is closely linked to unforgiveness is that of judgment, both toward individuals and toward groups of individuals. Matthew 7:1 says,

"Do not judge, so that you will not be judged! For in the same
way you judge, you will be judged."

Bitterness can be the root cause of judgments, as can arrogance,
which leads to assuming a higher estimation of ourselves than others.

Although we may believe ourselves to be tolerant and to lack
prejudice, it is worth looking deeper to explore whether we may have
actually come to view groups of people or individuals with an air of
condescension, skepticism, or worse.

Perhaps we have allowed ourselves to see a particular group—those
who are conservative, liberal, democrat, republican, Christian, Muslim,
Jewish, white, black, brown, Asian, and on and on our prejudicial list can
go—in an unrelentingly negative way. Perhaps that perspective has become
so ingrained that it goes undetected in our conscious thinking. Perhaps it
has been a family bias that has existed for generations. Perhaps we assume
that a particular group has no virtues and deserves to be considered
irredeemable.

When we are talking about groups like the Nazis or the KKK or
other groups whose purpose is to destroy and kill, then that assumption
is accurate in regard to the vision and objectives of that group. That
conclusion can be made when we accurately appraise things. Let me
point out, however, that hatred toward the individuals who ascribe to
the philosophies promoted by those groups are not to be included in our
assessment of "irredeemable."

Every person is redeemable, and that should be our hope. We may
need to ask ourselves whether we have formed bitter judgments toward
groups and how we might reframe our thinking and our posture.

When we are talking about a racial group, an ethnic group, a
political group, a religious group, there is no basis for lumping those
"individuals" into one assessment and deeming them all lacking, unfit,

hypocritical, or even evil.

I had personally found myself fearful and suspicious of people from a Middle Eastern background after the attacks of 9/11. It was an unfounded prejudice, but one that I had gradually adopted based mostly on fear. Certainly, there were self-proclaimed sects within those ethnic groups whose purpose was to kill and destroy. I had no business thinking of that group of people on a whole in that same light. We do well to examine ourselves regularly to see whether or not we have allowed ourselves to judge another group of people or persons individually in a bitter or arrogant way.

This would hold true in relation to people who are involved in certain behaviors that are clearly called sin in the Bible. While we can be clear in our understanding of sin in our own lives and the lives of others, we cannot have a condescending and judgmental attitude because of that sin.

We can speak into the lives of others when appropriate but always from the perspective of Galatians 6:1-4:

> "Brothers and sisters, even if a person is caught in wrongdoing, you who are spiritual are to restore such a person in a spirit of gentleness; each of you looking to yourself, so that you are not tempted as well. Bear one another's burdens, and thereby fulfill the law of Christ. For if anyone thinks that he is something when he is nothing, he deceives himself. But each one must examine his own work."

Often, there are significant judgments in church settings; we can be very hard on those who disappoint and hurt us within the church. Some have felt as though a leader has ignored or spoken harshly to them. Perhaps you have taken offense on behalf of another person that you feel has been handled in a manner that you disagree with. So often, this leads to hurt and judgments toward pastors, leaders, and other Christians in general.

While there may be sufficient evidence to fuel resentment and unforgiveness for past offenses, we are still hurting our own selves—and often others—when we choose to cling to them. Sometimes healing comes by allowing the right people access into our lives, instead of bolting the door to anyone who resembles the person or group of which we are suspect.

There are many Christians who need to be restored to the Body of Christ but are holding onto hurt and judgments. It would be liberating to be vulnerable in a healthy way and be a connected part of God's family again. Proverbs 18:1 says,

"He who separates himself is a fool and argues against all sound wisdom."

That sounds a bit harsh, but God understands the damage that happens when we put those "no access to my heart or life" checkmarks beside names of people or groups. Let wisdom and discernment lead you.

Is it possible that you may have written off the church or Christians in general because of something you or another was offended by? Has that offense or judgment helped you in your personal life and brought greater freedom to you or has it brought an underlying loss of peace? Would you be willing to consider rethinking your responses to previous offenses? Would you consider forgiving and releasing those you have an offense against?

Maybe, in your particular case, you need to have a conversation with someone within that church—even a pastor or leader. While attending the particular church involved may or may not be the right option, having a conscience free of judgment is always the right choice.

If we are willing to consider and examine the judgments that have influenced how we view people, I believe that we can trade them in for compassion, understanding, and mercy. I love what James 2:12-13 says,

"So speak and act as those who are to be judged by the law of liberty. For judgment will be merciless to one who has shown no mercy; mercy triumphs over judgment."

That is such a clear mandate for determining how we should look at others—free from judgment!

It is critically important to understand the difference between judgment and appraisal.

The Bible says clearly,
"Judge not, lest you be judged." (Matthew 7:1)
It also says,
"A spiritual man appraises all things…" (1 Corinthians 2:15)

What does that mean? It means that we have not only the right but the responsibility to examine and investigate all things, including people in our lives and those who have influence and authority over us, including all types of leaders—even husbands, bosses, relatives, etc.

We are not to be devoid of discernment or good judgment; but there is a clear difference between this type of appraisal and arrogant judgment. One is for the purpose of making educated and informed decisions about people and life issues. The other is purely for the sake of criticism, skepticism, or raising our own estimation of ourselves.

The fruit of appraisal is clarity, wisdom, and sound choices. The fruit of judgment is gossip, slander, unforgiveness, and separation.

So, by all means, be discerning and appraise well (with the right people in the right context), but let's avoid bitter judgments toward others, as they lead to sorrow and discord and are a form of unforgiveness.

Having experienced both spectrums in regard to calloused unforgiveness and judgments as opposed to releasing people from their intentional or unintentional offenses toward me, I've found safety, happiness, and freedom with the latter. I will continue to press into keeping myself free from unforgiveness and judgment.

Let me add that, for those in ministry, the willingness to continually examine our hearts in regard to these things is not optional. If we have developed skepticism toward people, we cannot truly love and care for them. We can pretend, but my motto is, "You cannot impart without giving your heart." Jesus opened His heart to those He ministered to. He called them his friends.

Let's be willing, for those of us in ministry, to refuse to close our hearts to others—no matter how many times we have been hurt, betrayed, or rejected. No one was more scorned or rejected by the people He came to serve than Jesus. He refused to give up on people. He refused to close himself off and harden his heart. He refused to allow past offenses from people He trusted to determine His willingness to love fearlessly.

My desire is to live judgment free and to love fearlessly. Join me in that pursuit!

CHAPTER 4

The Power of Embracing Others

This is one of my favorite topics, as well as one of my most abiding aspirations. I want to share with you how blessed I have been in regard to the mother God gave to me. I have written memoirs for my family about the unique and incredible inheritance I have been honored to have been given. While my father was not present, my mother was such an inspiration in every sense that I reflect on it with awe… realizing I have received the actualization of Psalm 16:6,

"The lines have fallen to me in pleasant places; indeed, my inheritance is beautiful to me."

This is true both of the inheritance that was granted to me in my mother's family line, but also in my inheritance with my husband, children, and grandchildren. My mother, as well as my grandmother, great grandmother, aunts, and cousins are rare and delightful people. Not only do they nearly all possess a deep, demonstrative faith, but they are generous, kind, gracious, and embracing. When I am in their presence, I feel welcome—I feel valuable.

My mother so exemplified this quality that, upon hearing a story of a visiting couple sitting next to her at church who had come upon hard times, she invited them and their twenty plus pets to come and stay with her. She was a single mom with a very limited income. She had been forced to work well over forty hours a week after my father left her; she received no income from him whatsoever. But, that didn't stop her; she invited them to come—lock, stock, and barrel. My mom took care of and helped this couple until they were able to make their own way—which happened to be several months later. She never complained or regretted it. She embraced it and them fully.

This is just one of literally hundreds of stories where my mom, willing to embrace people of all types and persuasions, came alongside and made an invaluable impact on their lives. She worked as a cleaning lady for many wealthy people, who ended up becoming some of her very best friends. They remained devoted to each other well into their nineties.

She had that effect on people. She loved fearlessly and embraced people, and they loved her back.

She was never without a large group of deeply devoted friends. Although she went through a dark valley for a while after my father rejected her for the woman who was my mother's neighbor and friend, she chose to forgive and to get better, not bitter. She threw herself into helping others, myself included.

I was blessed with eight children. They are the joy of my heart, and I am unimaginably thankful for them. However, when they ranged in ages from newborn to twelve—with three under four years of age, I needed help and lots of it. I honestly cannot remember a time when I would call my mom to ask for help where she would not find a way to promptly come to my home an hour away and begin cooking, cleaning, ironing, and other chores in earnest.

Everyone who has had the privilege of knowing my mom has been touched by the way in which she has given of herself to them and shown them unconditional love. She was the quintessential embracer.

Sharing that, it is obvious that I have some advantage in this area, having had it modeled so well for so long. But, it is a quality that truly allows people's defensive walls and hurts to come down—opening the door for real and lasting friendships. It demonstrates the unspoken sentiment, "I have room for you in my heart and life." I would recommend it to everyone. It makes life so much richer and more enjoyable.

Of course, being in the ministry for the last forty plus years, learning how to embrace people has been a trait that has helped me access their true feelings and needs in order to really come alongside them in a way that matters.

For my first job interview I was asked if I liked people. My internal response was much different than my spoken one, which was required in order to secure the job. Inside, I knew that I did not actually like or trust people—I was apprehensive of deep, trusting relationships, other than with a couple of my closest high school friends. God, in His relentless willingness to help me become more like Him, taught me how to embrace people with an open heart. He took my weakness and made it one of my greatest strengths.

I recall a time early in my marriage when Helena, a woman who I looked to as a mentor, called to share something with me that she felt God had told her. She told me that there was an area in my life that was fairly non-existent; it was void and without life. It was the area of love. I could have taken offense at that, but I chose to ponder it, trying to understand it.

She went on to say that God was going to make it the most fruitful area of my life, and I would be known as one who loves deeply and loves well. As the years passed, I saw that what she had spoken was actually transpiring. People would come to me and express that they knew that I genuinely loved them; it was apparent to them. God was doing something in me in the area where I was most barren.

The more I had learned to just follow that inner voice to reach out to people—my family, my friends, the people in my church, people I met along the way—the more I felt I was experiencing the actualization of the word that Helena had shared with me. It was becoming part of my DNA.

In many ways, it's like learning a new skill—like dancing or cooking or a particular sport: the more you practice, the stronger you become in that area. The more I just stepped out and embraced people, the more natural it became.

Let me be more practical when I talk about embracing. It means to take and enclose or encircle in the arms, to accept, press to the bosom in token of affection.

Take a moment to think how much it means to you to feel as though you are accepted and welcomed into someone's life and heart. Did you ever ponder the idea that people really need a place of refuge at times? We all need a safe place, where we feel like we can be ourselves and just relax, without the need to perform or be under scrutiny. Deuteronomy 33:27 talks about God's offer to be our refuge.

"The eternal God is your refuge; and underneath are the everlasting arms."

Another way to view it is to see the need for people to be nurtured through kindness. Proverbs 19:22 says,

"What is desirable in a man is his kindness."

How simple a concept, but how profound! I have heard people say that they remember a person's kindness more deeply than they even remember a sermon or an event. Kindness sticks in our hearts—it is like a suave applied to our wounds. It's refreshing. It lifts us up.

I have a friend who is a pastor's wife. Marion is a delightful person. She and her husband pastor a large church. I have known her for over fifteen years, but there is never a time when I am in her presence that I do not feel embraced and encouraged. Not only does she tell me how much she loves me and honors me, but she makes me feel like I am the most important person in the world whenever I happen to be in her area.

She drops everything she is doing and makes special time for her and I to spend together. She invites me into the lives of her children in a way that has created wonderful friendships with them as well. If she finds out that I'm coming her way, every effort to make sure I know I am valuable to her is made—special luncheons, dinners, coffee dates, etc. Not only does she embrace me in her heart, but she is deeply affectionate with me, and I never leave her presence without feeling like a queen. She has embraced me, and I am completely my best self when I'm with her. There's no need to ever be anyone other than who I am because she loves who I am and lets me know.

She has learned how to embrace people well. I know I am not the only one she treats this way—but when I'm with her, I feel as though I am!

Kindness is an instrumental part of an embracing heart. In Galatians 6:9-10 we see kindness encouraged, while also including the need to forgive.

"Be kind to one another, tenderhearted, forgiving one another,
as God in Christ has forgiven you."

Combining kindness with forgiveness is a formula for fearless love, which translates into being an embracing person. It renders our enemies helpless and without accusation. It often silences the harsh behavior of others.

"A soft answer turns away wrath." (Proverbs 15:1)

Paul draws attention to this type of kind, embracing posture in 1 Thessalonians 2:7-8,

"But we proved to be gentle among you, as a nursing mother tenderly cares for her own children; having so fond an affection for you, we were well pleased to impart to you not only the gospel of God but also our own lives, because you had become very dear to us."

That reflects the heart of a person who aspires to represent Jesus well—who knows that people need the touch of a gentle, affectionate person. He even goes as far as to say, 'a nursing mother'. Think about the way a nursing mother dotes on her child, giving her whole attention and care to it.

This is quite a statement: Paul compared himself to a nursing mother. If someone as straight forward and strong as Paul was can describe himself as having the characteristics of a nursing mother toward people in the church, we can achieve that level of gentleness and kindness toward those we are serving. It also reminds us again of God's nature—that is who Paul was emulating in this verse.

When we are emphasizing kindness, it is important to consider the wise instruction in Proverbs 3:3-4:

"Do not let kindness and truth leave you. Bind them around your neck, write them on the tablet of your heart. Then you will find favor and good repute in the sight of God and man."

Kindness mixed with truth is a wonderful combination; it lifts a person up while helping to offer a way of escape when needed. It is not afraid to speak directly about a problematic area, but it does so with humility and grace.

There is nothing virtuous or kind about pretending that all actions and behaviors are acceptable and that there are no moral absolutes.

Sometimes, kindness and truth require us to speak truthfully to a person who is treating us, others, or themselves in a poor manner. Sometimes kindness and truth require us to set the record straight where there are lies, gossip, or dissension present. Sometimes kindness and truth require us to make an unpopular stand publicly about a difficult issue.

Kindness and truth mingled and melded together in a perfect balance are reflective of God's character and have a powerful impact. Truth without kindness is mean; kindness without truth is meaningless.

We often don't realize how much of an impact we can make on those around us by welcoming them into our heart and by demonstrating good old-fashioned kindness to them. When Proverbs tell us that what is desirable in us is our kindness, it reminds me of how important the day to day ways in which we embrace others really are—we can bring hope and lift a person up with simple, kind deeds and words.

I encourage you to continue to learn how to embrace people with a kind heart, looking to be a safe and nurturing refuge. There are people in your sphere of influence that need you—they need your touch and your embrace!

CHAPTER 5

The Power of Encouragement

If you look around, you will see that people are drowning in a cut-throat culture that seeks to promote individual self, even if that means stepping on others. This can be so exhausting and deflating, and I find that there is a dearth of encouragement in the lives of many people I know, within and without the church.

If you look at the percentage of broken homes today, we can begin to understand how many have struggled just to survive their childhood and youth, let alone come out with a sense of well-being and confidence. I know in my own life, I had a mom who was one of the very best people I have ever known. Her heart was giant, and she helped anyone and everyone she ever met.

She died at age 93, with a large group of dear friends and admirers. I would not have traded the mom I had for any other one in the world—she left me with a legacy of selflessness and care toward others that is invaluable, and I loved her deeply.

In spite of her wonderful heart, she was not yet schooled in being an encourager in many senses of the word as I was growing up (though she was better able to bring affirmation to her many grandkids). I never once doubted her love, but I did not always feel greatly affirmed as a person or a young woman. Believe me when I say, she made up for it in a thousand different ways, but words of affirmation were not her strong suit, and I happen to have a need for words of affirmation. Most people who know me know that I would cite that as my primary love language—perhaps because I missed out on it early on.

So, from experience, I understand the great unfulfilled need for encouragement in the hearts of so many.

Having come to know God as my greatest cheerleader, I am able to draw from that well and now be a cheerleader for others. I know I can still learn much in that area, but I have grown a great deal throughout the last years of my life. A saying of mine—"affirmation overcomes hesitation"— has proved true in my life. There have been times when I was hesitant and even afraid to do something that I really wanted to do. The words of affirmation and encouragement from someone in my life gave me the inner strength to follow through and do it!

That is true in relation to writing this book; without a number of people encouraging me and reminding me that I had something of value to share, I would probably have neglected to actually write it. Encouragement yields tangible results.

1 Thessalonians 5:11 says,

"Encourage one another and build each other up…"

Encouragement can take many forms. It can be through sincere, affirming words or by showing honor in one form or another. It can even be demonstrated through undaunted acts of affection toward another.

I'll always remember my experience with a dear lady who was in her late seventies. I had attended a bridal shower at my church and was seated at a table with this woman, whom I had never previously met. During the course of our meal, she mentioned that she had never been given much physical affection in her life, leaving her feeling awkward about it.

In spite of that, she seemed comfortable and open with me and I had a sense that kind affection may actually be an encouragement to this dear lady. I can tend to be a bit bold in regard to jumping in where angels fear to tread at times, so I went with my internal instinct.

As I went to dispose of my dishes, I snuck around behind her on my way back and gave her a loving, warm hug. She seemed a bit taken back but not annoyed. I had secretly shared the message with quite a few of my friends at the shower to also consider giving her an encouraging hug. After about twenty or more loving and encouraging hugs, she was what I would call "tickled pink" with all the attention, affirmation, and warm encouragement. She asked if she could have a photo with all the kind people who had hugged her. We happily obliged.

Several months later, upon attending the wedding of the bride who the shower was held for, I ran into this dear lady and her husband. He approached me to tell me that the day of the shower had been one the most special days of his sweet wife's life. He explained that she felt somewhat unlovable and even afraid of affection, and our demonstrating kindness and tender affection toward her touched her in a very deep way and encouraged her heart greatly.

I was so thankful that we all were able to be a part of that moment for her. Another saying I've adopted—"affection counteracts rejection" has proven to be accurate. It was true in this story and has been the case in many others.

I was privileged to be able to encourage quite a few other dear ladies by just hugging them and showing them how lovable they truly are. Of course, we need to be sensitive and discerning, but sometimes people need what they are a bit unsure of how to receive. My experience has been quite positive in regard to demonstrating affection as a means of encouragement where I have felt that it is the right choice.

I often think of the prodigal son's father, who saw him coming afar off and ran and passionately embraced him, even though the son's last interaction with his father was one of bitter rejection toward him. The father did not allow that to dictate his willingness to show vulnerable love and affection for the wayward son. I think it is a valuable thing to disregard our own intimidations and to demonstrate true, perhaps unwarranted affection toward people.

I used to see myself as the returning prodigal in this story. My perspective now includes the desire to be the embracing father, while still realizing I am always in need of running back into the Father's arms. The father in this story symbolizes our heavenly father. The way He views and handles this wayward son is worthy of emulation.

I want to be a person who runs to the broken hearted, needy, guilty one—having been that person myself on many occasions. Every returning prodigal wants someone willing to run to embrace him or her and to help them take to heart what 2 Corinthians 5:18-19 says,

> "God reconciled us to himself through Christ and gave us the ministry of reconciliation, that God was reconciling the world to himself in Christ, not counting people's sins against them. He has committed to us the message of reconciliation."

It is worth considering whether or not we are willing to put ourselves out there in the area of encouraging others. It's easy to get caught up in our own struggles and think that we don't have anything to give. When we are looking for opportunities to encourage another person, we will certainly find them. The question is: are we looking?

Another vital need that many people have which we can meet is for sincere words of affirmation. First, the difference between flattery and words of affirmation is important to distinguish: flattery is defined as excessive or insincere praise given especially to further one's own interest.

Sincere—and that is the key—words of affirmation are not excessive, but rather draw from traits that we see and discern in a person that can be articulated for the sake of building that person up or honoring them.

It is a good thing, and not a phony thing, to look for people's strengths and call attention to them. When we are looking for this opportunity, we can usually find quite a few things to focus on that would emphasize their strengths. When we do this, our positive outlook can become part of their identity.

It is a lot like God calling me His "Crown of Beauty." I had not seen myself in that light, but He did and He chose to clearly and blatantly convey that perspective to me.

We all need encouragement. As I endeavor to encourage others, I also receive regular encouragement from trusted people in my life. I have two sisters, who both have a strong gift of encouragement, and they are always bringing to attention things about me or things I've accomplished and telling me how wonderful and well done they are. I am grateful for their kind words and have learned to allow them to truly penetrate my mind and heart.

There was a time when I would have shrugged it off and would not have been able to receive it, but accepting the unmitigated love of my Heavenly Father has changed that about me. I have learned to be encouraged by their words and let them do the job they were meant to do—bring hope and courage.

I tend to run many things I am writing or pondering by my sister, Paula. I know she will be honest, but she also makes me think I can conquer the world. She is a sincere and genuine encourager, and her words have power!

I have several friends who also have a great gift of encouragement. They call me up to be the best version of myself. They send me texts, cards and just plain tell me about the good things that God has put in me.

(You probably know who you are because I've told you!) I feel as though I can accomplish anything after being in their presence. They build me up; they strengthen my heart and hands; they empower me—just like God does.

Just simply paying attention to people is another way to encourage them. Some people see quality, invested time as a demonstration of great love and encouragement. When you choose to spend time with them, they feel as though they are greatly valued. When you notice them and acknowledge them and show them that they are worth your time and your friendship, it makes them feel like a million dollars.

In line with that, becoming an attentive listener is a big part of giving your attention and encouragement to someone. Have you ever been in a conversation with someone and they are very distracted—looking around, checking their phone on and off, looking as though they are lost in other thoughts? How do you feel when you've left that interaction? Like you were encouraged and heard and valued? Most likely, not so much.

Listening is a lost art that needs to be rediscovered. When we choose to engage in a one-on-one conversation with someone, let's actually give them our undivided attention. Let's let them know we really care about what they are saying. Let's not cut them off while they are talking.

How about when we are so busy pondering a clever response that we don't even really hear what they are saying? When we listen well, we stop processing other issues in our minds and actually try to hear their words and their hearts as well. We slow ourselves down and devote ourselves to that one person for the moments we are with them. Maybe we even act as if there is no one else in the room—we value them.

If we hope to give or impart things to others, we need to have equity with them. Equity comes through consistently demonstrating your interest and care for a person. Equity is earned and doesn't come cheaply. I believe we cannot gain valuable equity without being a caring, patient listener.

You have a gift you can offer to others; it is the gift of encouragement. We are made in God's image, and He is the ultimate encourager. He actually *"calls those things that are not as though they are"* (Romans 4:17). So, He sees things in us before we do. Wow! Him seeing those things causes us to see them in ourselves.

Don't withhold encouragement from others when it is in your power to give it. Don't let fear, intimidation, insecurity or jealousy keep you from using your invaluable influence to bring courage to another person. You can change a person's life by being an encourager—a cheerleader for them.

CHAPTER 6

The Power of Loyalty

Loyalty is another of those qualities that is both extremely valuable and also in short supply. The Bible promotes loyalty, knowing that it is foundational for building long-term relationships and is a trait that demonstrates strong character—one that God emulates Himself and requires from us.

Internally, people crave loyalty. Even in our culture, where it can seem to be a scarce commodity, we still promise to be faithful and true to one another in our wedding vows, as well as our oaths and vows as politicians, doctors, military—they all contain a pledge of loyalty.

Loyalty holds true when the circumstances are less than desirable and is very often proven in trying times.

A story comes to mind of a friend of mine who has weathered some difficult moments in the course of our friendship. She not only served as a wise and faithful member of my leadership team, but also is one of my dearest friends. During a very tumultuous season for our church, where many of her close friends had decided to leave the congregation, Karen remained loyal and steadfast.

When there was confusion about what was truth and what was fiction, she asked the hard questions and processed prayerfully before proceeding. She used great discretion in regard to whom she spoke and what she said. After using God's discernment and coming to a clear conclusion, she made a decision to remain by my side and would not be shaken in that choice.

During the years that we have been friends, there were times when she could have chosen an easier path with considerably less responsibility and conflict. But she saw her commitment to our friendship and her placement within the Body to be more covenantal than convenient.

I once asked her, "What would I ever do without you?" She replied, "That is something you will never have to find out." That is what loyalty looks like.

She was not the only person in our church who demonstrated this type of loyalty. I could tell many such stories of beloved friends who refused to be moved off course in spite of the whirlwind around us. Their loyalty encouraged me so very much. I was able to face a painful and tumultuous time largely due to their deep loyalty.

During those demonstrations of great faith and loyalty to me, I also experienced what disloyalty can do to the heart. In our particular situation, there were miscommunications that could have been resolved and mistakes that could've been corrected. However, beloved friends chose instead to react with distance and judgment toward me and my family. Efforts to resolve conflicts were refused; lies were believed and spread.

Even in the face of valid hurts and offenses on both sides, loyalty called us to give each other the benefit of the doubt, to hear each other's heart, to seek the truth and consider our response in prayer. Instead, actions were taken out of anger from a place of offense, and the loss of valued friendships caused great hurt for me and my family and for many others as well.

Distance and separation alone is not what defines disloyalty. In reality, sometimes a change in relationship is wise, necessary, and unavoidable. When we've appropriately and prayerfully assessed a relationship or situation and determined that we cannot remain in it while being faithful to God, that is not disloyalty.

Loyalty does not necessarily require a restoration to intimacy or a particular role between individuals. That is determined by the attitude and demeanor of the parties involved and their willingness to work toward that objective.

Disloyalty happens when we choose our own benefit, feelings, or plans rather than seeking truth, practicing forgiveness, and allowing God to guide the process. In the scenario I described, I believe that a positive outcome was certainly possible—one where misunderstandings could have been sorted out and precious relationships could have been retained.

So how exactly can one demonstrate loyalty in the face of conflict?

In the stories of Jesus and Peter, as well as of David and Saul, I believe the Bible gives us some insight for how to remain loyal, how to respond to disloyalty, and when to restore a relationship.

When Jesus was in the most vulnerable place in his earthly life, having been accused of blasphemy and other crimes and on the precipice of being sentenced to death, one of his dearest friends, Peter, demonstrated blatant disloyalty, betraying Jesus publicly, denying even an association with his once-beloved friend and lord. His disloyalty was a sharp blow to the heart of Jesus, but Jesus forgave him and restored him to a place of courage and faith.

Peter ultimately became and remained a loyal follower of Jesus, and was actually killed for that loyalty. The relationship was fully restored due to the disposition of both Jesus and Peter.

In contrast, the story of David's demeanor toward Saul in I Samuel illustrates the value of loyalty and how much God esteems it.

David was anointed by the prophet Samuel as the future king of Israel at a young age, but for many years after this anointing, Saul still acted as king, despite having forfeited that role due to his blatant disobedience toward God. King Saul was unpopular in the lead up to David's reign, and he often heard the praise his people lavished on David. Saul's jealousy ultimately provoked him to hatred for David.

Even though a young David had been used by God to kill Goliath, thus saving Israel, Saul could not bear the thought of losing his position and power to a younger man—one considered more worthy and valiant than he was. He attempted to kill David more than once and persecuted him continually.

David's response is both unique and reflective of loyalty and an excellent character. He said,

> "The Lord forbid that I should lay a hand on the Lord's anointed." (1 Samuel 26:11)

No matter how much he could have felt entitled to retaliate, he chose loyalty instead. Even when, after being pursued and threatened by Saul for months, he had a perfect opportunity to take Saul's life, he refused to do it—loyalty and honor was God's command. In 1 Samuel 22:14, Saul rebuked a priest for feeding David, but the priest replied, "Who of all your servants is as loyal as David?" David was known among the people as a man of great loyalty.

God rewarded David for his loyalty and integrity in 1 Samuel 13:14, where he told Saul,

> "But now your kingdom shall not continue. The Lord has sought out a man after his own heart, and the Lord has commanded him to be prince over his people, because you have not kept what the Lord commanded you."

God promoted David to the position of king when he was thirty years old.

Loyalty to Saul, but more so to God Himself, was a foundational trait that brought about God's appraisal of David and his eventual promotion. David had great faith in God's plan and timing. He knew that God had anointed him as king and was content to wait for God's timing to bring it to pass.

In David and Saul's case, restoration was impossible because of Saul's choices.

We can have a loyal heart toward another without being closely associated with them or continuing in our former roles. We can do our best to "maintain a pure conscience" and still be unable to have a trusting and vulnerable relationship with a person. I do not believe God requires total relational restoration as a part of loyalty. In the case of David, Saul refused to change his attitudes and actions, leaving David with no choice but to be on guard toward him and to remain at a safe distance.

Here are some other important things I've learned about loyalty:

Sometimes people relinquish loyalty toward others over matters that should not require such a step—such as political leanings and disagreements, theological differences, failures in morality and so on.

Let's be realistic...people will disappoint us. They will have moral failures. They will differ in their ideas and opinions from us. They will hurt us and offend us. They will gossip about us at times. But, does that require that we put that fateful mental checkmark next to their name that indicates that we have written them off and have abandoned any loyalty toward them? I don't believe so.

Loyalty can be defined as trustworthiness. Proverbs 20:6 says,

"Many a man proclaims his own loyalty, but who can find a trustworthy man?"

What a question that we can ask ourselves! To be considered trustworthy is an honor. It means that we are worthy of someone's trust— that they believe we will act with their best interest in mind.

Loyalty, or trustworthiness, lived out consistently gives us equity in the lives of others. As I have demonstrated loyalty in relationships, I have also been given trust and equity. Often people are willing to trust me with painful and even embarrassing struggles in their lives. They seem to truly believe that I will not toss them aside or think less of them even when I know their deepest, darkest failures. And, to be honest, their failures do not hinder my devotion to them.

One of the greatest deterrents to feeling the need to disengage from people who disappoint me is being aware of my own weaknesses. When I am able to step back and take an inventory of myself, I am able to be less hard on others. Realizing that I am deeply flawed truly helps me to be more circumspect when I appraise the lives and situations of others.

God's loyalty to me is not based on how well I have performed. It is not based on my merits but, rather, on the fact that I have chosen vulnerability and surrender to Him and have allowed Him to be my Father.

He takes care of His own and He takes care of them well.

Another practical way to demonstrate loyalty is by steering clear of gossip. Gossip can be disguised as "concern for another" and, sadly, is often a regular part of church life.

Have you ever had someone approach you, saying, "I am so concerned for so and so; did you hear what is going on with them?" That is often a way to open the door to share a bit of "spicy" gossip that they have come upon. Gossip never truly helps bring solutions and, ultimately, it interferes with the ability to have a loyal heart.

This was a vital lesson Keith and I learned early on in our preparation for ministry. As a newly married couple preparing to pastor a church, we sometimes had the occasion to visit ministers in their homes at meal times. On a few occasions, we observed the pastor and his family discussing the church members in an unfavorable light during their meal. They would go from person to person within the church, discussing their irritating mannerisms and habits.

We both learned from those times that we wanted to avoid that mistake. In our thinking, it would be hard to maintain a level of pure-hearted concern and care for people who we would be cynical and critical of. We made a decision that we would not speak negatively about the people in our churches—or people in general—in our home, even to each other.

The responsibility to appraise a situation or a person's actions was another story. Often, we would have to talk about how to handle someone in the church who was making bad choices, causing discord or had other difficult things going on. However, that does not mean that we had to talk about them in a way that was demeaning or critical.

Appraisal denotes assessment and finding empowering solutions. It does not denote arrogant judgment toward someone. This was a valuable and fruitful lesson that allowed us to see people with a lot of optimism, trying to troubleshoot regarding issues in their lives without scorn.

Another synonym for loyalty is faithfulness. The Marine Corps' motto is Semper Fidelis, which is Latin for *Always Faithful*. This motto is emphasized beginning in boot camp and throughout one's service in the Corps. In the course of the service of a Marine, one is often called upon to risk or give his life in order to save the life of a comrade. Knowing that their fellow Marines will stick with them and that they will never be left behind is part of the reason that the Marine Corp is one of the most effective fighting forces in the history of our country. Faithfulness (loyalty), and not just in a military setting, is powerful and has a profound effect in all relationships.

Two of my very favorite worship songs are "Great is Thy Faithfulness" and "The Goodness of God," which emphasizes the declaration that "All my Life You Have Been Faithful." The reason these songs emanate with me so strongly is that when I sing them I reflect on the fact that, no matter what I have walked through and how much I have faltered and proven less than worthy, God's faithfulness—His loyalty— has carried me. It has carried me from a place of victory, through storms and dark places, and then back to victory again.

He has always shown up for me and told me what the next step was. He has always held out His hand and provided a way of help and escape when needed. I am so keenly aware of the presence of that proven faithfulness and loyalty, that it gives me great courage when I face the next challenge.

Isaiah 41:10-13 says,

"Do not fear, for I am with you. Do not be dismayed, for I am your God. I will strengthen you and help you; I will uphold you with my righteous right hand. All who rage against you will surely be ashamed and disgraced, those who oppose you will be as nothing and perish. Though you search for your enemies, you will not find them. Those who wage war against you will be as nothing at all. For I am the Lord you God who takes hold of your right hand and says to you, 'Do not fear, I will help you!'"

Now, that is what I consider loyalty and faithfulness!!! I am encouraged and strengthened by that. I become fearless in light of that!

CHAPTER 7

The Power of Unity

Philippians 2:2 is a verse that has been foundational for building women's leadership teams in the churches we have worked with. Paul encourages the Philippians to...

"Make my joy complete by being of the same mind, maintaining the same love, united in spirit, intent on one purpose."

What a wonderful objective and visionary goal for us, overall and in our leadership teams—male and female.

I firmly believe that this does not just happen automatically in any group of individuals. It doesn't just happen on the job site, in the military, in a social club, in a family, or even in a church. Without leadership and calling people up to this place, there will undoubtedly be division and disunity.

It would be ideal if people could be unified just because they are part of the same organization or have a common interest or objective. It would be ideal if people could be unified just because they love each other. But, when you have two or more people together, you have the opportunity for disunity and discord.

Paul was letting them know that it would be a cause for much joy if the Philippians would endeavor to become of one mind, having the same love, united in spirit, striving for one purpose. I think this is actually an achievable goal; I have seen it happen in our midst within local churches. Once we learned how to move toward that end and began to practice the principles that create unity, it became our way of life. Our leadership teams became a cohesive unit as they joined efforts to help others around them.

In order to assure that we actually became of the same mind, we spent a great deal of time communicating and repeating our purpose and our intention to live out Philippians 2:2. We did trouble shooting and even practiced handling hard situations and conversations, so that we were in a position to know how to best maintain this ideal.

We committed to be honest and open with each other when offense came, as it certainly will amongst groups of individuals who spend time together. We made a covenant to confront one another in humility and kindness and to forgive one another when needed. We covered a lot of bases in our training in an effort to become a faithful and united team. Again, that outcome was achieved with a great deal of prayer, study, discussion, and instruction.

Unity is a result of people who spend time together for a particular purpose ("intent on one purpose") and then follow through with the steps necessary to maintain this condition.

If you have been to Chick-fil-A (and who hasn't!), you will observe the unified way in which the employees handle and treat their customers. That oneness of purpose was brought about through consistent training that is universal among all Chick-fil-A restaurants. There is a vision statement, a training program, and a requirement to stay the course in regard to these things.

Employees are not permitted to choose another style or vision and do their job as they see fit. If they don't enjoy being polite to customers, they don't have the option to employ an individualized method and speak abruptly and impatiently with the customers they are responsible for, or to offer sloppy service. Everyone does it the same way—with excellence and courtesy. If the employee is unwilling, then they are not suited for that job.

Unity is critical to their vision statement: "To glorify God by being a faithful steward to all that is entrusted to us. To have a positive influence on all who come in contact with Chick-Fil-A." I can say assuredly that, without clarity and unity of vision, purpose and conduct, they would not be able to be a positive influence to all who come to Chick-Fil-A.

The same applies to your local church. Without clarity and unity of vision, purpose and conduct, the church will struggle to have a positive influence upon those attending and upon the community. In the process of training leaders within any organization, it is vital to call them into that place of like-minded vision.

I have seen church leaders who think that it is overbearing or prideful to require their teams to be in step with them and to follow their lead in regard to vision and specific ways of doing ministry within the church.

While no leader should be arrogant or condescending in any way, it is not unhealthy or inappropriate to give strong and clear direction.

It is important to set the standard of service and direction within the church. Isaiah 62:10 says,

> "Go through, go through the gates, clear the way for the people. Build up, build up the highway. Remove the stones and lift up a standard over the people."

This is a clarion call for leaders to go before and clear the way by removing obstacles and lifting up a standard for the people. In other words, create a way for people to walk a path that is not strewn with chaos, bitterness, gossip, and cattiness. Instead, create a standard or a vision to follow that is clear and life-giving. Lift up a banner that brings security, purpose, hope, love and unity to the people in your sphere of leadership and ministry.

Once a group has become established, they become spreaders of that healthy DNA to the rest of the body.

2 Timothy 2:2 says,

"The things which you have heard from me in the presence of many witnesses, entrust these to faithful people who will also be able to teach others."

Committing God's relational and ministerial wisdom to faithful men and women in a way that truly creates unity and purpose only comes through intentionally choosing, preparing, and establishing those same people.

When teams are thrown together without the specific effort of connecting them with shared goals and strategies, they are unlikely to be effective.

One of my daughters experienced this outcome after traveling to another country to teach for a year. She was asked to come and volunteer her time and talents, but after arriving, it became apparent that there was to be very little training for any of the volunteers in their roles as teachers at this school. She had to learn as she went and felt at a loss regarding direction and clarity of vision, as each teacher planned out the year without oversight.

She had come to serve and to do her best to teach these young students, but it was a very arduous task due to the lack of unified purpose for the project.

I remember her telling me one time, "Mom, I wish you could come and teach these folks how to train a team of leaders; they are so disconnected and ineffective. We don't meet together for discussion, training, or even friendship. We're on our own." Without a clear call to present the purpose and rules of conduct for this team that had come from several different states to help, everyone just tried to do what they felt was right.

On the opposite spectrum to my daughter's experience, I recently attended a program to help with an ongoing struggle I've had with losing weight. I committed myself for a month to exercise, eat healthy foods, and to become more mindful about my eating habits.

One of the first things that was evident when I arrived was the overarching, consistent vision that was presented in every part of the program. It was evident when you did an exercise class or a nutrition class or ate a meal in the dining room.

Someone had clearly defined a vision for this program and everyone who worked at this center had to completely adhere to and embrace that vision. If they were unable to, they would have to find another occupation.

Not only were all the employees and managers on the same page, but everyone who participated in the program was required to follow certain rules and protocol. Rather than following my own path, I chose to become part of a plan—a standard that was given—in order to see a positive and successful outcome. The result from this seamlessly unified presentation of vision was that things ran smoothly and excellent results were achieved. What if everyone was able to make their own rules and do their own thing while they were there? It would yield chaos and be a fruitless endeavor for those involved.

Interestingly, many people who attend a specific church feel as though they should conduct themselves by their own rules and their own agenda within that church. They sometimes balk at being told that there are any requirements at all. This does not provide security or unity, but rather a fragmented group of individuals, usually accompanied by strife and confusion.

I have found that unity in a church is powerful. It provides a safe place for those who have been scarred and beaten up in their daily lives at their workplaces and even sometimes in their homes. When this type of purposeful unity exists, it is accompanied by the "same love" Philippians 2:2 refers to.

So, instead of wondering when someone will criticize them, ignore them, or gossip about them, people know they will be esteemed and treated with respect. They understand that a Philippians 2:2 vision creates an oasis of peace in which they can learn and grow. They realize that, instead of a loosey-goosey, anything-goes atmosphere, they enter into a prepared place where a standard of love, purpose, and unity has been promoted. What a refuge for women and men!

What a place to unload the stress of the chaos and mistrust they have experienced in other parts of their lives. This is something to strive for and to build in our churches.

CHAPTER 8

The Power of Pursuit

When I have had the opportunity to speak at women's meetings or conferences, one of the teachings that I have often shared is one I've titled *Peace through Strength in Relationships*. Peace through Strength is a term I first heard when Ronald Reagan was president. He believed that our best foundation for peace as a nation was through strength—strength in our military, strength in our economy, strength in our unity as a people. He stated,

> "We know that peace is the condition under which mankind was meant to flourish. Yet peace does not exist of its own will. It depends on us, on our courage to build it and guard it and pass it on..."

He understood that peace in any area requires diligence and pursuit, not apathy and a *"whatever happens, happens"* attitude.

Relationships take a lot of work and diligence in order to be strong and peaceful. When we are willing to make them a priority and to take the initiative, our relationships can bring incredible joy and blessing to our lives. I have found this to be the case in my life, but it has not been without setbacks and struggles.

I have a wonderful relationship with each of my children, but it was sometimes hard fought. There were many moments and even days when I felt like stepping back and actually did because I was hurt and felt rejected due to misunderstandings.

Having found the courage to press on and pursue these precious people in my life, I found that fighting for those relationships was not only completely worth it, but it helped me to become more mature and step further away from the fears and wrong mindsets that tried to control me.

I have met so many people who have been willing to hold onto feelings of hurt or rejection rather than to pursue peace with a person they love. Yes, we all have those moments where we need to perhaps step back or be alone or regroup. But, sooner or later, we need to pick ourselves up and pursue the people in our lives that God has given us to love.

Family and friends are not expendable—they are part of what makes up the fabric of our lives. Of course, relationships are not without difficulty. They are often seemingly impossible. When we refuse to be a pursuer, we are destined to lose many of those relationships due to neglect or misunderstanding.

I have seen husbands who desperately love their wives, refuse to pursue them, thus allowing the relationship to become cold and dead. The same holds true for wives. If someone would have taken the initiative to pursue the other person in order to find a solution, restoration would have been possible. We can be stuck so deeply in pride that we would rather watch our marriage be ruined than humble ourselves and pursue a person we actually love.

I have watched parents become disappointed and angry with their children, refusing to pursue a relationship with them any longer. This is so painful for both the parents and the child, whether or not it is obvious on the outside. Sometimes the rift is never healed and the pain that it causes cripples those involved.

Pursuing people, whether or not they deserve it, is a quality that comes from God. He pursues us when we don't deserve it. His love cannot help but pursue us. He is not willing to just let us drift away from Him or to be lost to Him. When Adam betrayed Him, God came looking for him:

"But the Lord God called to the man and said to him, 'Where are you?'" (Genesis 3:9)

As I've mentioned in other chapters, some relationships are perhaps irreparable. When there is a person in your life who has been abusive, destructive or threatening, you are dealing with an entirely different dynamic. Those types of relationships require great caution, counsel and discretion and do not fall under the same recommendations for pursuit. The relationships I am referring to in this chapter have potential for restoration and soundness.

You may think that, being a pastor's wife, I have not had to fight hard for my relationship with my husband; in reality, I have. I came from a home without the presence of a father, and as I've explained, I had a deep sense of insignificance. My husband came from a broken and dysfunctional home as well; his mother was married six different times. He was moved from home to home, school to school, and step-father to stepfather, many of whom were not kind to him. His own father showed very little interest in Keith throughout his entire life.

So, when we decided to be married, at the age of twenty-one, we were without any real model to draw from. Needless to say, the battles that ensued were quite difficult. As a minister once told us, Keith was dynamite, and I was nitroglycerin: an explosive combination.

Pursuing one another, when we felt like throwing in the towel became a necessary and frequent act of surrender. We knew we loved one another, but we did not always like one another. I recall praying on my knees many times and asking God for the courage to either apologize or just even approach Keith with gentleness and humility. To be honest, there were times when I felt like it was almost impossible to choose humility and pursuit—I was just too hurt. Those opportunities bring out the worst of our insecurities, but help us to become a person of internal strength.

I have found that pursuit in relationships has become part of my DNA. I realize that relationships don't happen on their own; someone takes initiative and reaches out or pursues the other person. Many people are timid in these areas, so I often decide that I need to be the pursuer.

We may tend to assume that another person is uninterested in a friendship with us when, in reality, they are assuming the same thing about us. They are reluctant to be a pursuer due to their own insecurities. There is a verse, Numbers 13:33, that I used to quote to my children when they were feeling intimidated about facing a particular situation. It says,

"We were like grasshoppers in our own sight, and so we were in their sight."

When we begin to demonstrate insecurity and intimidation in a relationship or situation, others pick up on that fear and begin to view us in the same light. In this story in Numbers, the people were feeling small and incapable in light of the giants they were facing. When they projected that, their enemy began to see them as small and incapable as well.

It's a spiritual principle and even scientifically proven that, when we emanate self-deprecation and lack of respect for ourselves, that's how we are seen by those around us. However, when we choose a faith-filled assessment of ourselves, others see us in that light. If we choose to see ourselves in light of God's ability working through us, we can pursue relationships without fear of rejection. Rather, we courageously look for opportunities to connect with and befriend others.

Back to my *Peace through Strength in Relationships* teaching—I love to use acronyms when I teach, because they help me to stick to specific points. So, I opened this particular teaching with the acronym P.E.A.C.E. The P stands for Pursuit. Pursuit in relationships is something that takes us beyond our own apprehension, shyness, and fear of putting ourselves "out there."

To pursue is to follow with a view to reach, to attend to. There is no apathy in this definition. Rather, it describes a willingness to look for solutions, resolutions, and an intention to reach or attend to another. If we choose to be a pursuer, we assume it is our responsibility to build and even restore relationships, when at all possible.

Psalm 23:6 says,

"Surely His goodness and steadfast love will pursue me relentlessly all the days of my life."

Wow! He pursues us. He seeks us out. He even pursues us relentlessly. Relentless means determined, unflinching, unyielding. This is how He pursues us to demonstrate His love and care for us.

I want to be more like Jesus: I want to be a relentless pursuer, even when it is painful, awkward, and precarious. How about you?

Also note that this verse highlights the fact that He is pursuing us with His immovable, unchangeable goodness and love—not His anger or vengeance. If we have eyes to see, we will find this theme repeated over and over in the Bible.

I have had some interesting opportunities to become a pursuer in regard to people within our church. In one scenario I recall, there was a young woman I had spent time counseling through some addiction struggles, and she became offended with me based on some things she believed I felt about her.

As soon as I realized this, I texted her and called her in an attempt to try to repair things and make sure she knew I had no desire to hurt her at all. She did not answer, so finally I went to her apartment and knocked, but no answer. I proceeded to sit outside for several hours waiting for her to answer the door or to perhaps come out. She finally did, and I was able to sit down outside with her and to make sure she knew that I cared for her and did not want to be at odds with her.

Thankfully, we were able to go forward with no division between us. That is a somewhat extreme case, but I wanted to make sure, if it was in my power, that we were at peace in our relationship.

After the church split that I have mentioned previously, I wanted to find a way to connect with those who had left the church, in order to make sure that they knew I did not hold bad feelings toward them.

One day in particular, I was shopping at Walmart and happened to see one of the ladies who had left, several aisles away. As I kept her in my line of vision, I proceeded to steer my cart in her direction. She saw me out of the corner of her eye and averted her gaze, but I was not deterred. I went right next to her, greeted her, and asked how she was. I also inquired about her husband, who had recently had a serious health problem. She responded nicely and gave me an update.

Before I left that several-minute conversation, I gave her a hug and told her I loved her. She responded with, "I love you too." Although we did not see each other after that day, she knew I held nothing against her, and I hope I opened the door for her to forgive me for my shortcomings as well.

I also wrote cards and notes to others who had left during that time and told them all the things I appreciated about them when we were working side by side as part of the same church body. I invited many of them to coffee or lunch just in an attempt to bring a sense of healing. Some accepted, and some did not; however, I did not want to leave any loose ends of unresolved, unpursued, broken relationships or deep hurts. I recently saw another woman who had left during that time, and we were able to connect in a warm and meaningful way.

I have to share one story that is not so pleasant. There was a couple who had moved away and who had remained annoyed and frustrated with us. I didn't have occasion to see them and neglected to pursue the wife, who had once been a close friend. After several years, she died suddenly, although she was only in her thirties. I cannot tell you the grief I felt when I realized she had died and I never had an opportunity to talk with her and to tell her how I felt. I loved her very much, but had not pursued her as I could have or should have. When I found out that she had died, I wept for hours at having lost that opportunity to be restored to a dear friend.

Pursuit is so important and often yields wonderful results. Pursuit is a life-long endeavor.

There were times when I had to pursue a person after I had handled them in a way that was unacceptable. One such time, I had found out that a woman who was new to our church was gossiping about how my husband and I were handling helping a family within the church that needed both practical and financial help. Apparently, she disagreed with specifics on how it was playing out. The things she was saying seemed incredibly unfair and uncalled for.

I approached her after church and gave her a severe tongue lashing, telling her we do not gossip in our church and she was completely out of line. I went home from church feeling rather proud of myself for having set her straight.

After a couple of hours, I began to ask myself, "*Why would I take the liberty to call her out so harshly and sharply?*" I realized that I was not bringing correction in the way that 2 Timothy 2:25 instructs us,

"In humility correct those who are in opposition..."

Yikes! There was no humility in that interaction.

I called her and told her I was very sorry for the way in which I had spoken to her and that, although I still held to the fact that we shun gossip in our church, I should have explained that to her in a much better way. She accepted my apology and even asked if I would consider mentoring her and helping her mature in some areas. I told her I would.

So, in the times when I have misspoken or handled people roughly, I have attempted to follow up by making amends for my brash behavior. That is a part of pursuit.

This quality or ability does not just come naturally for me. Having a background of living under the cloud of insignificance, the ability to pursue others in relationships is something I needed a lot of reassurance and assistance from God in. In earlier times, I had sometimes approached an opportunity for a relationship with a preconceived idea that the individual I was considering reaching out to would probably not find me very interesting and, thus, may shun or reject me.

It's amazing how God can radically change something inside of us, as I usually approach relationships now with great expectation and as an opportunity to make a new friend. I go forward with the assumption that the person will most likely be happy to know me and be my friend. I am then free to look for ways to get to know them and to come alongside them in a positive, helpful way. That is a change only God could make, and I love the fruit of that mindset.

I look at it this way: if God is willing to relentlessly pursue me with the goal in mind of reaching and attending to me, should I not attempt to follow His lead? Even though I still have some intimidation in this area, I have learned how to turn my back on it and to speak an applicable Bible promise over myself. I usually speak it out loud, sometimes very quietly when I am in the presence of others.

Sometimes it's necessary to confront our fears in the midst of the battle and speaking out loud—even with a whisper—words of faith that declare that God has me covered, will chase away that intimidation. I remind myself and declare that *"my gift makes room for me"* (Proverbs 18:16).

I would never have been able to go from a person who fears people to one who pursues them without using the weapon God gave us—His Word!

I find that speaking God's Word—specific applicable verses—over myself and the situation can turn things around miraculously. I cannot overemphasize how much this particular practice has changed me and many, many outcomes I've had. Had I not applied God's promise to my frailty, I would have stepped back and let that frailty overtake me. God's Word has power to change us and our situations.

Before we had children, I had gotten a job as the administrative assistant to the president and vice president of our local Christian television station. I was in my early twenties and when I walked into the office for the first time, a wave of fear and intimidation hit me. *"They are all great friends and I'm new—I don't know if I will fit in"* was the general idea of the thoughts that were loudly speaking to my mind.

I remember turning away from everyone and whispering, *"You surround me with favor as with a shield, Father"* (Psalm 5:12). I knew I needed God's help to overcome my fear and I really did believe He would do what was promised in that verse if I didn't give up. Before my first day at work was over, I felt the fear lift and a sense of God's confidence and favor fill my heart instead.

I ended up enjoying that job more than I could say and made some wonderful and precious friends there. I felt God's great favor throughout the several years that I worked there. I have learned to utterly and completely rely on Him and His promise to give me courage and to turn me into a pursuer.

I want to be a pursuer like God is. He is looking to reach us and to attend to us in every way. Let's allow Him to give us great confidence and courage through His promises in order that we can be fearless about pursuing others in order to come alongside them and help empower them.

If you have experienced intimidation or fear in pursuing others, I encourage you to speak God's promise over your life and your circumstance. You will be amazed at the outcome. I have gone from passive to pursuer because of His ability working through me.

CHAPTER 9

The Power of Vulnerability

Vulnerability is one of those subjects that makes some people feel very uncomfortable. By vulnerability, I mean the willingness to be honest and open about ourselves, including our personal frailties and struggles and to allow people access to us as real human beings—not a perfect, plastic version of ourselves.

The definition of the word vulnerable includes the connotation of leaving yourself open for criticism or even attack. It's true that, when we are unguarded and refuse to be anything less than authentic, there is a risk of people looking at us in a critical light.

Let me clarify what I don't mean when I talk about vulnerability. I don't mean leading with our insecurities or weaknesses. I don't mean self-defacing and self-deprecating perceptions that are readily expressed. I don't mean exposure of delicate information to the wrong persons who have no need to know our deep personal information and who may not handle it with wisdom.

I do, rather, mean the willingness to face the fact that we are all weak and lacking in one way or another. We are all in need of assistance and repair. Therefore, it is not shameful to be open to the appropriate people in our life about those very areas of lack.

I have taught a lesson entitled "Facing our Frailties" on

several occasions. The target audience for this teaching was church leaders. Why? Because there is an unspoken mandate upon those individuals to protect their reputation in a way that keeps them from getting help in an area when they may most need it. Vulnerability can be a frightening thing for them.

However, I believe that the willingness to be honest about personal struggles can help leaders to avoid falling into the trap of sin that will derail and ruin their life's work and purpose.

I believe that we can be open and willing to disclose our needs and to just put ourselves out there in a positive way. It is incumbent upon us to be genuine and to get counsel, encouragement or even intervention when we need it. I do not believe that pastors, pastors' families, leaders and people in general, should suffer in silence and simply "bear up" under conditions and situations that need to be addressed and adjusted.

A pervasive secretive posture can keep us imprisoned in a failing marriage, failing relationship, or a failing church.

Often, pride keeps us from seeking help when things are falling apart around us. Sometimes children of leaders in the church feel the responsibility to use extreme discretion in talking about any struggles or issues within their home, but are not given a safe outlet where they can process through these things. There is an unspoken code of silence that they know must be followed at all times. This leaves them in a very difficult position.

There must be a safe place where leaders within the church can be vulnerable and honest without fear of reactive repercussions. While leaders and their families are wise not to air their struggles casually, it is so very important to create a way for them to seek counsel and help. A pastor I know is associated with a reputable Christian psychologist. He has made sure that his wife and family know that they can call this psychologist at any time to discuss any problems they are dealing with, including problems that center on the pastor himself.

The Bible makes it clear that we, as Christians, have inherent weaknesses and will continue to have them as long as we are residents of this earth.

In 2 Corinthians 12:9 we read,

"And He has said to me, 'My grace is sufficient for you, for power is perfected in weakness. Most gladly, therefore, I will rather boast about my weaknesses, that the power of Christ may dwell in me.'"

It appears that Paul is not opposed to revealing that he has weaknesses.

Even more so, he said he wants it to be clear that, in the face of his own personal weaknesses, the power of Christ takes over and brings that power to bear in relation to the frailties that exist in Paul's life. He said he wants to brag about that fact! Thus, I can risk being me, which includes my strengths and my weaknesses.

When we act as though we always have it all together, not only are we not being untruthful, but we are presenting a false standard of perfection that others feel they can never attain.

There is a fine line between discretionary disclosure and indiscreet divulgence.

There is no virtue in blatantly revealing personal issues for the sake of appearing humble or just because we feel insecure about those things; however, there is virtue in humbly confessing our sins one to another in a manner that is honest and looking for assistance.

The book, *John Wesley's Class Meetings: A Model for Making Disciples*, tells how they formed the basis for accountability and friendship in the early days of Methodism. One of the standard practices was that of small groups meeting regularly to pray together and encourage one another.

During those meetings, people who attended would confess their failures and sins to one another, which is actually spoken of in James 5:16,

"Confess your sins to one another and pray for one another so that you may be healed."

The early Methodists took that very seriously, and they faithfully and vulnerably opened their hearts by revealing their sins to each other. The leaders in the movement were not exempt but, rather, were the first to open up about their own struggles.

Humility and vulnerability are signs of a good leader; they are not weaknesses.

This practice of confessing our sins to one another not only allows us to maintain a blameless conscience but also protects us from accusation that comes when secret sins are exposed. Being vulnerable and real as a leader, even about our failures and frailties, protects us from those people who may want to expose us in a destructive manner. Numbers 32:23 says, "Your sins shall find you out." I would much prefer to be honest about my weaknesses and sins, like the early Methodists did, than to have them eventually exposed in a way that creates great problems for myself and others.

There came a time when I needed to get some very real, practical help in regard to the weaknesses I have referred to in this book. I went to a wise Christian counselor, who helped me to process my ideas and to change some incorrect thinking patterns that were hindering my life and my role as a wife, a mom, and a leader. While I didn't tell everyone I ran across, I certainly did not feel as though I had to hide that information. I wasn't ashamed that I was getting counseling. I was not afraid to willingly share that I was seeking help to work on problem areas in my life.

Part of the blessing of having a team around you that knows you and is loyal and discerning, is the ability to share your life with them— the strong and the weak parts, the happy and the sad. They were accountability partners, prayer partners, and cheerleaders.

The amazing thing is that, when you are vulnerable with others in a discerning way, they do not respect you less but, perhaps even more.

Was there ever a time that information that I shared with others was misconstrued and used in a negative way? Yes. To be vulnerable is to be at risk of being hurt, but the benefits outweigh the risks. For the most part, those I opened my life and heart to were able to help me become a better version of myself—believing God alongside me for victory and growth.

I don't like plastic relationships that are superficial and keep everyone at a safe distance.

I realize that there are all types of friendships and relationships: some are more focused on mentoring or helping others; some are more focused on learning from others; some are more about mutual fellowship and enjoyment. There is a level of vulnerability that is appropriate for each of those types of friendships. We have to learn what that looks like and conduct ourselves accordingly, without the fear of being humiliated, rejected, or demoted.

Vulnerability is a trait that makes us more human and more relatable to others. It also brings a freedom in ourselves to rely on Jesus' strength to cover us and help us in the presence of our weaknesses.

May I be so bold as to ask—even if you are a leader, a pastor or a pastor's wife—if you have been afraid to be vulnerable and get help in an area where you are struggling. Maybe your marriage is painful or even disintegrating. Maybe your children are feeling the weight of watching their parents and themselves suffer in silence, with no remedy in sight.

Maybe you have felt that the code of silence is required to be a good leader and that it's not worth the risk to open up your life, including your frailties, to others who may be able to help.

I am not suggesting that to do so is without risk. I am suggesting that getting counsel, help, or intervention may be the very thing that saves your marriage, your family, your church or even your life.

The old pattern of protecting ourselves at all costs is, in my opinion, unhealthy and destructive. You, like me, may need to hear from someone with expertise in an area of weakness for you.

If you are reading this book and are in a place of crisis or near crisis, I would conclude that God is reaching out to you to get help! Find the right person — a trustworthy, wise person—and be vulnerable. Ask for help. Ask for prayer. Ask for counsel and wisdom. We need each other, and leaders are not excluded.

CHAPTER 10

The Power of Friendship

My mom used to tell me as a child, *"Make new friends, but keep the old; one is silver and the other gold."* Friendships are a treasure—whether they are friends we've had for years or ones we've just met. Proverbs 17:17 says,

"A friend loves at all times."

Most of us have had the joy of having at least one true friend in our life, who has listened, encouraged, and stuck by us through thick and thin. I have been blessed to have many such friends.

Pam, the very first friend that I made after coming to Christ, has stuck by my side for over 45 years now. She has been with me through so many joys and sorrows, and I with her. She was present at the birth of one of my children and sat quietly and prayerfully in the room near me when my mom recently went to be with the Lord. She has seldom missed a birthday party for my children and spends many holidays with us. Her friendship has brought so much into my life. She has included all of my family in her friendship and my children adore her.

I have had many friends within the churches that we have been a part of and have pastored, and have considered them very dear and close friends. I cannot even imagine how much less rich and happy my life would have been without the sheer joy of these friendships.

I have often heard that becoming friends with the people in your church is an unwise mistake for pastors and their wives. I cannot reconcile this idea with the fact that the Lord of all people, the owner and ruler of the Earth, has chosen to call you and I His friend. Howbeit that He can willingly call us friends, but we feel an obligation to deem ourselves on a different playing field or level from those within our congregation? I can't see it!!

Some people have been unfairly hurt and rejected by people they deemed as friends—some, very close friends. Thus, there can be an unwillingness to allow people to have similar access—fearing the same thing will occur. Sometimes, we end up tolerating people, managing people, surviving people.

I have heard the saying, "I love the people in my church; I just don't like them." I'm not sure how this statement makes sense. I would not enjoy pastoring people I don't like. The kind of love that is described in the Bible does not support that idea. Whether it's 1 Corinthians 13, that describes love as honoring, trusting, hoping, and persevering in a relationship or Romans 12 that reminds us to "Love from the center of who we are; don't fake it...be good friends who love deeply," there is a discrepancy between these two ideals.

True friendship, within the church and otherwise, is something consistent and genuine—it's not phony or forced. But it does require work and perseverance. Again, how telling is it that God Himself, who epitomizes perfection, is willing to embrace very flawed people as His friends.

In James 2:2, we read,

"Abraham believed God, it was reckoned to him as

righteousness and he was called the friend of God."

That verse tells me a couple of things. One, when we take God at His word regarding us and our circumstances, He views us as righteous. Two, Abraham was called the friend of God. Why? Because He spent time with God and He believed what God said; thus, God considered Him his friend.

I love the story of how Moses would go out to the tent of meeting and spend time with God. They would talk about many things—including issues that would affect the whole nation of Israel. Exodus 33:11 says,

"Thus the Lord used to speak to Moses face to face, just as a man speaks to His friend."

Now that is something that I want to cultivate in my friendship with God. What a thing to be said of us! It shows us how God desires to relate to us and it's quite amazing.

In John 15:15 Jesus said,

"No longer do I call you slaves, for the slave does not know what his master is doing; but I have called you friends, for all things that I have heard from My Father I have made known to you."

There again, Jesus Himself told us that He considers us to be His friends.

Just from these three verses, and not including the many others that contain similar sentiments, it is clear to me that God values the idea of friendship and that, if He considers me to be His friend, I should also consider those in my sphere to each be at least prospective friends, depending upon their willingness.

Of course, discernment is necessary in all relationships. Some may ask, doesn't friendship require that we reveal our most intimate struggles and personal issues to those we consider friends? Of course not! But, that is covered in the understanding of overall discretion.

Doesn't friendship with people require that we spend a specified amount of time with that person regularly? No, friendship goes beyond the perimeters of the amount of information we divulge and even the amount of time we are able to spend. Friendship, rather, comes from sharing of our hearts and lives in a way that embraces and allows people in—even sometimes allowing them access to our frailties and failures, while using discretion.

Let me say, however, that sharing our husband's, family's or other's weaknesses would not fall into that same category. There are appropriate times and places for seeking counsel for those relational struggles.

Some of my closest friends are also my children. As they were growing up, my role was obviously that of a parent; I was responsible for helping to teach and train them. Even in the midst of all that entails, my hope was to plant the seeds of friendship in the interactions between us. I endeavored to treat them with the same characteristics that I speak of in this book, although many times I wasn't entirely successful in that aim.

As they got older, the time to let go of the authority aspect of my role in their life came. At first, I struggled to relinquish it. I thought that I had earned great equity and that meant that I could cash it in at any moment to exert pressure on them to follow my aspirations for them. What a rude awakening to learn that they had come of age and I no longer was the person who would be directing their choices and their decisions.

I remember my twenty-something daughter asking me, "Do you want to be an authority figure in my life or my friend?" It was a good question. I had clear ideas on what I thought was best for them, but it really wasn't my choice anymore; it was theirs. They had become adults. My role had changed and I had to acknowledge that and acclimate accordingly.

Throughout the years of their lives as young adults I found myself constantly learning through trial and error about how to be a friend—a good friend—to my adult children. I had to figure out how to deal with the things that they said that were offensive to me. Those closest to us have the greatest potential to hurt us, so when they were sharp or even defensive, I took it very much to heart. Many times, I stewed over it for days or even longer.

It took time and persistence to finally become a devoted and faithful friend to my children. One of the things that I had to learn was to let go of judgments about their actions, choices or decisions. I am willing to listen and offer advice when it is asked for. I still want to influence them with love, representing God's heart toward them. But that influence cannot be pushy, critical or demanding; rather, hopefully it can be demonstrated through model and, of course, input is always available when requested.

If I could somehow put all the difficult lessons I've had to learn in this part of my life in a compact written form, I would do so in order to help others avoid my mistakes. But, my overall message would culminate in urging parents to release their children into God's care and to be the friend God has empowered you to be—coming alongside them in the best way that you know how to.

The gift of having my children—each and every one of them—as a very close and valued friend is something I do not take for granted—I treasure it! Learning the hard lessons, often through their helpful input to me, has been challenging but so worthwhile. I'm sure I still have plenty to learn and I will endeavor to open my heart to those lessons.

The influence I have with my children reminds me of how we are influenced by God's Holy Spirit. He doesn't push His way in; He gently makes a way for us to hear His heart and His wisdom. We are always given the opportunity to choose whether or not we will respond. Of course, we often face hardships when we ignore sound wisdom from Him, but those are things we must learn on our own—without a parent or authority figure making the decisions for us.

Romans 12:9-10 calls on us to,

"Love from the center of who you are; don't fake it... Be good friends who love deeply."

Friendships are formed through faithful cultivation and nurturing. To have friends requires that we show ourselves to be friendly. We need to be embracers, forgivers, pursuers—learning through each season in our lives.

In the course of our friendships, it is important that we are not overly possessive, but rather look to practice the definition of friendship: attached to another by affection, kind, favorable, disposed to promote the good of another. The temptation to hold our friends too closely—in a way that doesn't make room for others at times—is a very real temptation. Our insecurities can show up in friendships and, while that is unavoidable, it's always good to allow our friends liberty to be close to others also.

Being a good friend isn't always easy, but it's wonderfully rewarding.

The characteristics that I cover in this book lead to strong and genuine friendships. Friendship was invented by God. He calls us friends. He pursues us. He embraces us. He encourages us. He is loyal to us. He forgives us. He teaches us what it looks like to be a good friend. When we are open, giving ourselves to friendships—all types of friendships—we are truly and deeply blessed and fulfilled. My hope is that the words contained in this book help you to have strong and vibrant friendships that last a lifetime.

CHAPTER 11

The Power of Having a Team

I'd like to begin by saying that, although my experiences have been with women, the principles in this book and this chapter apply to both men and women. Having a team of leaders who works alongside you in your service to God and His Church is invaluable. It is one of the most effective endeavors I have ever been a part of.

I have had wonderful opportunities to invest in women throughout my life, particularly over the last twenty years. Not only have I had the privilege of investing in the women—my beloved daughters—in my family, but I have also been able to build a team of like-minded women within our church, who I affectionately called the Dream Team.

At the time, I thought the title was unique and clever and suited them perfectly, because they were a dream come true, both in the way they served the church and in the way that we all related to each other. I still have a photo that we made of the 1992 USA Olympic Dream Team with their faces replacing those of the athletes. Now, over fifteen years later, I see Dream Teams everywhere I go; I guess we were ahead of the times.

All of the other chapters in this book lay the foundation for the conditions that must be present in building your own dream leadership team. The attributes that I wrote about were affirmed and strengthened as I worked alongside my team. They challenged my thinking, provoked me to be a better person, and helped me to practice the characteristics that are necessary in strong relationships.

The idea of building a team of women to help in the leadership of the church began after I spent a weekend with a pastor's wife in Louisiana who had already trained her own team of women. I was invited to attend a retreat with them and was very impressed with their devotion to one another and their heart to serve the vision of the local church as a unified team. They strategized, prayed, laughed, and enjoyed being together. That impression would not leave me.

When I returned home, I spoke regularly with my husband about creating my own local church team. I prayed, pondered, and discussed with Keith at length before finally formulating a plan to begin such a team. Thankfully, he never tired of our early morning coffee strategy meetings, where I excitedly ran all of my ideas and plans past him. He was a great sounding board, and empowered me to run with the vision God had put in my heart.

Just a note for husbands here, it meant the world to me that Keith took my role alongside him so seriously. He was very interested in my ideas and always took the time to make me the priority of his day. There was an extended season where I was deeply engaged in not just planning, but implementing the training and activation of this team of women. It is so important to think as a team and to value the ideas of the other partner in that team—whether wife or husband.

I have spoken to quite a few leader's wives who, when I asked them how their husband viewed their role or part to play, responded with a surprising, "We don't really discuss it." It was so necessary for me to have Keith's interest, support, time, investment, advice and affirmation in the process of carrying out my mission. So, may I encourage you to take the time to reason and process together in order to find the best way that your gifts and talents can be best utilized. You are meant to flourish best as a unit and when functioning as such, bring an element to any family, church or organization that is powerful and wonderful.

My first step, after having Keith's agreement and processing through some initial ideas with him, was to consider my objectives for such a team, and they began to solidify as I sat in front of my computer, asking God for a strategy and an outline to convey that strategy. My foundational objective was to duplicate myself, as is encouraged in 2 Timothy 2:2,

"The things which you have heard from me in the presence of many witnesses, entrust these to faithful men (and women) who will be able to teach others also."

My previous leadership template within the church was one where the pastor's wife would be responsible for the lion's share of women's ministry, calling on others here and there as needed. There had been no definitive plan or training methodology for bringing other women into that place alongside me. After experiencing the effectiveness of the team in Louisiana, I deeply wanted to have a team around me, one that would be able to minister to the women in the Body with the same heart that my husband and I had toward them—even better, with the same heart Jesus has.

I started by formulating some requirements and character traits that would be necessary in order to be part of this team. This led to a teaching, where I used an acronym from the first four verses in Isaiah 61. That passage talks about our ability to receive the anointed ministry of Jesus in our lives and to be healed, set free, made strong, and given his crown of beauty in place of our ashes (there is that reference to a crown of beauty again!).

But in verse four, it begins to talk about our responsibility as a result of receiving the healing qualities described in the first three verses. It explains that God wants to help us with all the struggles and heartaches and brokenness we deal with. Then He wants us to help others in that same way—coming alongside them as His ambassadors. I love having the opportunity to befriend and encourage someone.

I chose the acronym **T.R.E.E.S.** as a reference to Isaiah 61:3, where we are referred to as oaks. **T** stands for teachable, **R** for restored, **E** for established, **E** for equipped, and **S** for servants.

Those were the initial attributes I was looking for in a team that would serve alongside me as my right-hand people. I asked them the following questions:

Are you **teachable**? Will you be humble enough to take the time necessary to learn from me (weaknesses notwithstanding) and to allow me to speak honestly into your life?

Are you willing to be **restored**? Will you open your heart and life and be vulnerable enough to allow God and sometimes me into your pain, wounds and frailties in order to see them healed?

Are you **established**? In other words, are you planning to be planted within our local church or do you have plans to move to another church if you become offended, bored, or something similar?

Are you willing to be **equipped** by investing considerable time and dedication to learn how to care for people? In those days, the bar was pretty high—lots of training meetings.

Are you willing to **serve** others faithfully? This team was not about having your own special ministry or position; it was, instead, about caring for, embracing, forgiving, encouraging, loving others sacrificially—usually without recognition, without salary, without notoriety.

As you can see, this is a tall order. I wasn't sure if many of the people I initially invited to join me would actually buy in. I invited 22 women to come to the first meeting, where I laid out my objectives, vision, and plan. It was an ambitious one. We would meet weekly on Sunday afternoons for 90-minute classes.

I explained that it would be important for them to attend every week and only miss when absolutely necessary. Ultimately, all 22 women signed on for this daunting task. I had presented the overarching vision on our first meeting and then gave them two weeks to pray, discuss with family, and consider whether this was something they actually wanted to pursue. I asked for a letter from each of them letting me know if they were "in" and why they had chosen to be a part of this.

I honestly didn't expect the willing responses I received, but it showed me how much these lovely women wanted to be part of something bigger than their own selves. They were ready to invest in others. I am not suggesting that other people who are building a leadership team should require a 90-minute weekly training session for one year, but, somehow it worked for us. After the first year, we continued to meet regularly—sometimes weekly, sometimes every other week.

Throughout this process, I worked hard at communicating with them as a group and as individuals, making sure that they understood how much I loved them and cared about their lives. To be as effective as possible, we collectively decided to shrink the group to twelve, and ten of the women were assigned to work alongside one of the core 12. They did so with a great attitude and willingness to give their all.

As part of our training, we worked on all types of things, including practical ways to handle and eliminate gossip. We had a policy where we would hear a person out in regard to any offense they were struggling with. There were times when the issue was not genuinely caused by someone else but rather needed to be resolved within the heart of the offended person; but if needed, we asked the offended party to go directly to the other person involved within three days. After that time, we would check in with them to assure that they had followed through and resolved the issue.

This was a wonderful tool to not only squelch and eradicate gossip, but to bring resolution to the issues that were at hand. Their issues were not ignored, nor was the person shamed for struggling with their feelings about others—even if their feelings were about the pastor, worship leader, other church members, or me.

They were taught how to deal with offense Biblically, according to Matthew 18:15-16 (MSG),

"If a fellow believer hurts you, go and tell him--work it out between the two of you. If he listens, you've made a friend. If he won't listen, take one or two others along so that the presence of witnesses will keep things honest and try again."

In my experience within the church, unfortunately, I have seen gossip ruin many teams and even churches. Someone gets offended and then begins to vent to a friend or acquaintance. Before you know it, many are offended. I have seen gossip grow to a point where the entire church split apart and people on both sides were left broken-hearted and disillusioned. Proverbs 16:28 says,

"A perverse person stirs up conflict, and gossip separates close friends."

Yes, often people have legitimate concerns and grievances that need to be heard, considered and rectified when at all possible. But gossip is not the avenue by which to rectify them. There is a better way. I call it honest communication. It is the ability to go directly to a person who we have an offense with. There are ways to do that which are effective, and they need to be employed—using kindness and humility are always key.

Being vulnerable and expressing hurt or confusion over something said or done is both healthy and wise. It's vital that we go with the objective of seeing restoration, not just for the purpose of venting. Therefore, we should be emotionally prepared when we go, rather than approaching the person when we are still very angry. The person should know that we are approaching them because we care about the relationship.

I recall a situation that took place shortly after we began the second church that we pastored. I was saying hello to a friend and when greeting her toddler, I shortened her name to include only the first syllable. Apparently, she did not want her daughter referred to by anything other than her full name. She firmly rebuked me in front of a few other members of the church.

I was so surprised because I was being light hearted and warm toward her little girl. I didn't really answer her; I just slowly slithered away. After I was alone, I began rehearsing the conversation over and over, reliving the embarrassment and hurt I felt. I'm sure I shed a few tears as well.

After a couple of days, I began to think about how much I valued my friendship with this person. I deeply cared for her and didn't want to lose her friendship. I decided the best thing I could do was to forgive her, but also to go to her and tell her how I felt about her comment. I did actually feel that she should not have spoken to me in that manner. So, I worked up the courage and went to her privately.

I started by telling her that her friendship was precious to me, and I didn't want anything to interrupt it. I told her that I was trying to be warm in regard to her little girl and I didn't understand why she was so firm and harsh with me.

My opening comment about the value of our relationship opened the door for her to understand that I was not just trying to lash back at her but, rather, was wanting to assure that we maintained our warm friendship. She apologized and the conflict was forgotten.

I learned a valuable lesson that day that has stayed with me. I have made it a habit to go to people who have legitimately offended me and to talk to them directly. Instead of soliciting pity and the "ear" of a third party, I prefer to speak face to face with the person themselves, in order to bring clarity, forgiveness, and restoration. I can assure you that this path, though it may be hard to initiate at times, is the most reasonable and reliable one.

Most every personal offense that I have been willing to handle in this manner has turned out well and has had the effect of keeping the relationship intact—sometimes even stronger than before. Of course, the way we approach it certainly comes into play. But if we follow through, with kindness and a right motive, the outcome should be favorable. That is not guaranteed; there are people who stubbornly refuse to resolve an issue or to humble themselves. In those cases, we have to allow them that choice and see if perhaps they will come around eventually. They may and they may not, but we have an obligation to go to people according to Matthew 18, rather than taking the backdoor approach of gossip. I've taken a great deal of time on this topic because it's importance cannot be overestimated.

Conflict resolution in any relational setting is so vital. Improper ways of dealing with conflict in a church setting create havoc and heartache. We can save ourselves so much trouble and dysfunction by following sound principles in resolving conflicts. Practicing these principles and teaching them to those in our church greatly enriches our church life, as well as our personal lives. We were able to deal with even the most difficult disagreements by honestly, vulnerably and willingly talking—face to face—with an end goal of unity and cooperation in mind.

As a leadership team, we worked on why it is important to remain consistent and established. We talked about permanence in church membership, rather than being easily removed from our church family due to trivial matters. Having been in the ministry for over forty years, I have had occasion to observe many folks who go from church to church on a whim—not willing to put down roots and to become established.

I have a dear friend who pastored for many years. I remember one Sunday when he was speaking at Living Hope Church, he held up his pictorial church directory. He was illustrating how our churches can struggle with a lack of permanence in the mindsets of our members. He illustrated the change in his church membership by putting an X over those who had left during the course of a period of ten years. Of the 210 original family photos, 187 had been crossed out. That seems to be indicative of a lack of covenantal permanence and an unwillingness to resolve conflict well.

Of course, there are times when changing churches is necessary, but it should not be the consistent pattern we live by. Being a faithful, committed member of a church family is healthy and a sign of maturity, and it enables us to put our hand to the plow and make a long-term difference in our church and our community.

We talked about personal lifestyle and character issues, including marriages, parenthood, and relationships. We allowed each other access to our struggles and our personal shortcomings, using each other as a sounding board and being honest about the right responses.

We became the dearest of friends and the hardest of workers. We laughed together, cried together, served together, and even vacationed together. It's interesting that when you work hand in hand in the trenches, it forms a deep bond that is lasting. We formed our Dream Team over twenty years ago and are still the best of friends, even though my husband and I no longer pastor that church and live an hour away.

Another great outcome of having this type of team came when we turned our church over to a new pastor and his wife. The Dream Team came alongside them both with loyalty and willingness to serve. They understood the big picture and, although they missed us very much, they knew how to adapt and look toward building the local church under new leadership. Because of that commitment, they have grown to deeply love their new pastors.

A defining verse that describes my passion and hope for the women of our church and for women everywhere is Philippians 2:2,

> "Make my joy complete, by being of the same mind, maintaining the same love, united in spirit, intent on one purpose."

That, most definitely could have been our vision statement and, in my heart, it was. I spoke of it often with the women of my church and encouraged us to continually move in that direction and resist and deal with any and all obstacles that may hinder that outcome.

We studied and practiced hearing from God. I encouraged each of my team members to begin to journal, specifically asking questions to God that required an answer. They learned to trust what they were hearing and writing and became confident in the soundness of those words.

If you do not journal, I'd like to recommend it to you. It has helped me a great deal in learning how to pray specifically and to record what I hear God saying to me. It also is a great way to keep track of answered prayer, as well as instructional and encouraging words. I often go back and read my journals from 20 years ago; they remind me of what I was learning then. They help me to stay on track with the principles that are part of who I am.

I also encouraged my team to speak publicly. They studied and prepared well and brought wonderful truth from the Bible to others. I'll never forget the time a beloved team member spoke about the infilling of the Holy Spirit at a weekend conference we had. I literally had never heard a more concise or compelling teaching on what it meant to be filled with God's Spirit. They grew in their giftings and in wisdom.

They learned to counsel women well. I would sometimes initially accompany them to a meeting with someone and just be a backup for them. If I felt that they needed to adjust their counsel, I was not afraid to share that with them afterwards, in order to further empower them in their ministry.

They developed a wonderful demeanor about serving others in the church. One time, Darlene, a member of the Dream Team, said to me, "I count it such a privilege to have an opportunity to influence women in the church in a positive way. Thank you for helping to prepare me and for opening doors for me to be able to effectively do that." She felt honored to serve and to faithfully be a part of a team that cared for others.

Each week, most of the members of this team led a life group, consisting of five to fifteen women. They taught them, stayed connected to them, served them in practical ways, followed up with them and loved them well. I called them pastoral assistants, because they were able to accomplish so much within the church—making sure no one was overlooked and each person was personally cared for. They greatly enlarged the work that one pastor and wife could have done within a church.

When we had a church event, they would lead the way in regard to preparation—decorating, planning meals, inviting people and so much more. I had team members like Wanda, who was a one-woman event planner. She would make sure everything was done in excellence and nothing was left to chance. Her attitude was always one of willingness and servanthood. Women's events within the church became organized, efficient and effective.

We brainstormed together and, as a team, came up with ideas and outreaches that would encourage women—within the church and in the community. Their input was invaluable and their creativity never ceased to amaze me. We had spa nights, church sleepovers, and Hawaiian luaus. We had prayer meetings, Encounter weekends—where people were able to process through hurts and struggles in their lives in a redemptive way—and worship nights.

Every year, as a team, we planned a big Christmas dinner for all the women in the church and the community. It was a wonderful night, which featured a catered meal, singing waiters (the men of the church), candle light, beautiful Christmas decorations, lovely china, and an encouraging message. Each year, my friend and team member, Lynn, would lead the work on planning the meal and making preparations. She would ask me in the fall each year, "So...is it time for me to start planning for the Christmas dinner?" Even though it was an incredible amount of work, she did it with a great spirit and a lot of laughter—she made it fun!

The working relationships that we shared were so empowering and uplifting to me. I knew I had people I could call on at any time and who would be willing to help me as I served alongside Keith. They were well trained and carried the same DNA as we did.

I cannot overemphasize the value and joy of having such a team. Working alongside and living life with this team and with the people of the churches that we have pastored has been one of the greatest and most rewarding opportunities and blessings of my life. They say that being a pastor's wife is one of the most difficult roles there is. I have not found that to be the case. I believe one of the reasons for that was the Dream Team.

As a team committed to being of one heart and one mind, they readily allowed me to speak into their lives. I was willing to be honest with them and share things that were even uncomfortable. This need for uncomfortable honesty was more the exception than the rule, because they were absolutely incredible women with strong personal character, who I deeply admired and respected. They also had access to speak to me about concerns, frustrations, ideas, etc.

Sometimes other pastor's wives would ask me, "How can you be so close with your team and have them still maintain a level of respect or honor?" Frankly, that was never an issue. We all deeply respected one another and fostered that in our ways of dealing with each other and with other people as well. I never doubted that they respected me. They never doubted that I respected them.

I did carry myself as a leader. I was not afraid to lead with strength at times, but I also was very open to their advice and wisdom. I have a well-founded belief that a team can become one of the greatest tools possible in any endeavor. If done well, the people within the team support one another, help one another, and challenge one another—often quite seamlessly. There is a trust and a bond that serves the objective of sacrificial service well. It is a much lesser version of being in the military together, or perhaps playing on a sports team—a kind of "one for all and all for one" mentality.

My husband once shared that the Dream Team was like the glue that held our church together. He stated,

"The Dream Team has been used by the Lord to bring blessing to virtually every facet of our ministry. Their commitment to Christ, each other and the Kingdom—as exemplified by their radical commitment to Living Hope Church—is a foundational piece of who we are and what we do! They are dependable, sacrificial and caring. Their character makes them virtually unstoppable as a team. Several years ago, while our church went through a great shaking, the

Dream Team consistently rose to the occasion, filled in gaps and helped stabilize the ship. They gave Penny and I much needed encouragement and love--they inspired our church to keep moving forward. These teams cannot be built on a program agenda; they must have the same type of generous love and concern for each of the members that Penny has demonstrated time and time again--whether with the team as a whole or one on one. This is what it means to build by relationship and purpose!"

Because this team made such a deep impact on the church and on every facet of our ministry, they were actually a catalyst for writing this book. I learned so much about relating to people and God's character through working with my team.

I would recommend establishing a team to everyone—male and female—who is wanting to make a positive long-term impact within their organization.

It may seem like a daunting task, but if you establish your objectives and a strategic plan in advance and present it to the people you are considering as team members, it is both a doable and extremely rewarding endeavor. Follow through with discipline and vision. Presenting a vision to your team is a must—they will want to be a part of something that has a distinct purpose and agenda. I reiterated the vision of our team regularly, in order to keep us on track.

There is so much more than I have shared in these few pages to the making and the function of our Dream Team. I could talk for hours about the joys, the victories, the lessons, and the positive impact of this wonderful team, but I will end by saying, it is a worthwhile thing to consider whether or not a team that you are able to train, love and serve with is viable in your church or organization.

If you need further assistance, I am including my email address in this book and will do my best to help you. I wish you great success in this endeavor.

Closing

In closing, I want to say that I hope that this book is an encouragement to you. My life has not always been simple, but it has been exciting and very rewarding. Whatever place you find yourself in, the principles and character traits that I've spoken of will bring great joy and blessing to your life and will help you to touch and influence others in a wonderful way.

We are living in pretty uncertain and sometimes scary times. There are few things that are unshakeable. But, the faithful love of God is the greatest constant I know of. By living under and demonstrating His *Love, Leadership & Influence*, we can touch people in every walk of life and truly make a difference in their future.

Don't ever think that you are not able or cut out to be an influencer. You were created by God for favor and for purpose. The closer you stay to His heart, the greater your ability to offer His goodness to those you know and meet.

God has put eternity in your soul. He has a plan for people on this earth; that plan includes knowing Him as our greatest ally, our dearest friend, our safest refuge, and our wisest instructor. He is our creator and wants us to trust Him enough to fully surrender our lives, our futures, our dreams to Him. He has never disappointed me—not in the 47 years that

I have called Him my father.

If you have never surrendered your life to the one who made you and knows you better than you know yourself, there is no better time than now to do so. The Bible tells us in John 1:12 that,

> "To as many as received Him, He gave the right to become children of God, to those who believe in (adhere to, trust in and rely on) His name."

That verse describes what happened to me, at the age of seventeen, when I was aimless and angry, without any assurance of what my future would hold.

I knelt down and I called upon Him in a genuine way, expressing my desire for Him to rescue me and to teach me how to live. I asked Him to forgive my former selfish ways and I told Him that I surrendered my will and my ways to Him. I asked Him to be my Father forever.

From that moment on, everything about me changed. I truly became a new person. My attitudes, ideals and objectives began to change and I began a journey that led me to the place where I am captivated by His love and want to share it with everyone I meet.

If I can be of assistance to you, my email address is momala777@ gmail.com. Thank you for taking the time to read my first ever book.